I0691041

the punch
m a g a z i n e

ANTHOLOGY

OF

NEW WRITING

SELECT SHORT STORIES BY
WOMEN WRITERS

Edited and Introduced by
Shireen Quadri

NIYOGI
BOOKS

Published by
NIYOGI BOOKS
Block D, Building No. 77,
Okhla Industrial Area, Phase-I,
New Delhi-110 020, INDIA
Tel: 91-11-26816301, 26818960
Email: niyogibooks@gmail.com
Website: www.niyogibooksindia.com

Text © Punch Magazine

Editor: Upama Biswas
Design: Shashi Bhushan Prasad
Cover design: Misha Oberoi

ISBN: 978-93-91125-31-8
Publication: 2021

This is a work of fiction. The names, characters and incidents portrayed in it are the work of the author's imagination. Any resemblance to actual persons, living or dead, events or localities, is entirely coincidental.

Printed at: Niyogi Offset Pvt. Ltd., New Delhi, India

Contents

Introduction

Shireen Quadri

When we had invited submissions for *The Punch Magazine*'s first anthology of short stories in May 2019, the world was steady. There were no inklings of the imminent strange and dark times, no intimations of the solemn and sombre mood of the world in the wake of the outbreak of the coronavirus pandemic in less than a year. There was an overwhelming response to our call for submissions, with writers from several parts of the world, including the US, the UK, Canada, Spain and Russia, sending in their stories. After we whittled the list down to 18 stories, we had planned to bring out the anthology sometime in 2020, to begin the new decade on a new note.

However, Nature had its own plan. Early in 2020, just when we were starting the process to get the anthology ready for print, the world was interrupted, with Covid-19 upending several dimensions of our lives. There was an upside though. As we retreated indoors and into ourselves, the power of fiction to transport us to another world, another reality, revealed itself to us anew. During the lockdown, as the world slowed down, the love for reading seemed to be back; online sale of books registered a surge. In isolation, as we practised social distancing, we rediscovered reading as a therapeutic form of escape from the terrible reality of the present, from the doldrums of despair.

If the pandemic separated us, reading stories brought us closer, binding us together in a shared personal and intellectual chord. Stories, the world discovered once again, had the power to connect across divides; it offered us a way to heal, rebuild, reconfigure and reclaim our lives. The act of telling and reading stories was linked to our empathy, studies had suggested earlier. In the new normal, reading stories seemed to open the door to several possibilities—of understanding ourselves, of grasping the world.

A remarkable aspect of the short fiction published by *The Punch Magazine* since its inception has been its range and depth. Along with some fine works of poetry, in the past four years, we have also published an eclectic range of short stories by writers around the globe. Since we invite submissions from short story writers cutting across genres, we tend to receive entries that traverse diverse grounds. When we had conceived the anthology, our idea was to showcase a selection of the best works of short fiction by both male and female writers across continents, in line with the core ethos of the magazine that publishes writers from all over the world. However, once we were making the selection, we discovered that most of the stories had been submitted by women—mostly from India, but also from the US, the UK, Europe and North America. The stories by women had a distinct poise and panache. They reflected a certain kind of sensibility and sensitivity. Thematically, too, they were bound together by a unifying thread that weaved the concerns and preoccupations of individuals both within and outside the precincts of home. They spoke to our times, rampant with disparity and divisions—the way we live, the way we love. Circling around the ties that bind us and the relationships we build, they betrayed a deep understanding of the form and its numerous and wondrous possibilities. They also had a strong emotional core and a unique moral fibre. In the stories by women, to borrow a phrase by Eudora Welty, 'less was resolved, more was suggested.'

It was then that it occurred to us that the anthology had essentially shaped itself into a compendium of new writing by 18 contemporary women. Since we didn't have a theme, as that often entails restricting the writer to a set course, the entries we received hum with the cadences of different cultures and traditions, and unravel in the metaphysical or psychological realms. The stories in this anthology are deeply steeped in the cultural moorings of the places they are set in, often laced with the writers' lived experiences. They thrum and throb to the rhythm of the daily life of their protagonists—their inner struggles, existential angst and anxieties. They reflect on the universal human emotions and conditions. In some stories, we get to know the way memory works. In some other, we discover how the present echoes with the past, and feel the palpable nostalgia for good old days. There are stories that centre around the memories of early crushes, unforgettable first loves and adolescent romance, and others that dwell on the passage of time, with all its attendant ravages—loss, suffering and decay. There are stories that concern themselves with family history and present a portrait of a loved one, and others that capture the vestiges of despair at the gradual disappearance of a way of life or markers of culture. A couple of stories are also rooted in family traditions, interlinked either with food or honour. Alice Munro and George Saunders have told us how we become a different person after reading a short story, how we come out a little more aware and a little more in love with the world around us. Neil Gaiman has described a short story as the 'the ultimate close-up magic trick' that either takes us around the universe or breaks our heart in a couple of thousand words. The stories we zeroed down on for the anthology did all this: took us around the universe, made us fall a little more in love with the world and also broke our hearts—all this in a mere three thousand words. Having emerged from their writers' observations of and confrontations with the chaotic realities and unequal order of the world, these stories wrestle with the genial human follies and peculiar frailties, the psychological and emotional conundrums, the misery of the human condition and the perilous journeys we make for a better life— essentially, all that is fundamental and fascinating about our existence on earth.

Ameta Bal's 'Static A.D.', with its first-person narrator engaged in the act of looking within, resonates with the themes of isolation and loneliness and the need for us to take refuge in stories, let stories define us, form us. It also underscores how we stitch together our multiple selves and identities. 'My family's accumulated story formed the fabric on which I've patch-worked my own half-assed life experiences,' voices the unnamed narrator at some point in the story, which is also an eloquent meditation on the passage of time and a rumination on the end of the world. Anila SK's 'A Tale of Disconnect' begins in a district court in Colombo and flashes three decades back to Kerala in the early Eighties—a woman, given to speaking 'a language no one understands', tells the story of her dysfunctional marriage and, in the process, the 'silence' of the gods, who never answer her. In 'Pandemonium,' Anjali Doney tells a tremendously enchanting story of unrequited love, set in Cochin in the early Eighties, which heaves with the innocence, sweetness and heartache of unfulfilled college romance—the flush of emotions, the rush of hormones. In Camilla Chester's 'Terms and Conditions', Laura Pimpleback, a 36-year-old single woman, stuck in a mundane, dead-end job, flits between reality and dream, and finds one of her most cherished wishes come true. Geetha Nair G's 'Falls' tells the story of two classmates studying in Delhi, who are drawn to each other as much by their lost state as their common love for literature, but eventually grow apart, and cross paths again, briefly, 30 years after they were in love.

Just as it occurs in 'A Tale of Disconnect' and 'Falls', the interplay between the past and the present and, in some cases, how it has a bearing on the future of the narrators/

protagonists is a common strand that runs through several stories. This interplay often involves family—what holds them together, what pulls them apart. In 'Olya's Kitchen' by Helen Harris, the narrator, Nicholas, works towards keeping alive the memory of his deceased grandmother. Three stories revolve around Kashmir, 'the paradise on earth' that continues to spawn narratives of pain. In Humra Quraishi's 'Kashmir Valley's Soofiya Bano' that draws on the flood fury of 2014, the waters bring a son back to his mother from the police custody. Meena Menon's 'The Closed Cinema' laments the shutting down of a cinema hall on the busy Lal Chowk road in Srinagar. Shilpa Raina's 'The Vacation' is an ode to the courage, resilience and fortitude of the wife of a Kashmiri Pandit, who steers her family through depravity and loss as they live in a state of permanent exile.

Driven to the edge, human beings are capable of going to unimaginable extent. In Latha Anantharaman's cleverly told and delicately structured 'The Very Narrow House', set in Palakkad (Kerala), the reclusive family of a sub-priest at the temple has a dark secret that must be guarded fervently. Jayshree Misra Tripathi's 'Indigo Blue' employs the device of 'story within a story' to explore both parallels and dichotomies between past and present. 'Is the imagination unbound in its possibilities of rebirth, past lives woven in a kaleidoscope of memories, snatches of conversation, once spoken or perhaps overheard?' wonders its narrator. In Meher Pestonji's charming and darkly hilarious story, 'Ghost', 10-year-old Kaizad, who loves playing pranks and acting ghosts to scare his little sister, unwittingly invites trouble for the family. Tammy Armstrong's 'Artichoke', set in Rome, foregrounds the flawed approach to a researcher's quest to understand painter Caravaggio (looking down upon those who found their way in his works) as opposed to his co-traveller who sees in his subjects the faces of the tourists milling around, the faces of the street hawkers—'just ordinary people in extraordinary moments.' A young man, the son of a widower, in 'The Dance of the Happy Muse' by Rinita Banerjee, must seek temporary solace in art when family responsibility feels too heavy to bear. For Purna, a washerwoman in Rochelle Potkar's 'Honour', set near Mahalaxmi station in Mumbai, family responsibility is something she drowns herself in, day in and day out. In Sarah Robertson's lyrical 'Marietta's Song', the magic notes of a magical song—'enough to lift the dead along into a world of passionate flight, with pre-dinner martinis every night'—played on piano by a miracle man following a royal decree at an asylum for a Norwegian resident with dementia, makes the narrator believe both in miracles and love. In Vineetha Mokkil's 'Sunday, Bloody Sunday', the narrator, a young woman, finds all hell breaking loose after she announces that she is in love with a man of another faith. Lastly, in 'Crossing', Vrinda Baliga delves into the dehumanising ordeals of illegal immigrants who must navigate the choppy waters of the sea in a rickety old boat, harbouring the hope of a new life elsewhere. Some of them will make it beyond the mythical borders of the sea, but it will not be without its costs.

After we had selected these stories, giving each submission a close, careful read, finalising a publisher to get the anthology printed was another tough task. Since this was going to be our first anthology, there was a lot of expectation riding on it. We chose to pitch this to Niyogi Books, known to bring out books with a lot of passion. Established as a boutique publishing house with an impressive line-up of well-produced coffee-table books as well as fiction and non-fiction titles, their commitment to publishing good books resonated with us.

While making the selection, we read and reread several of these stories. They made us think and are going to travel with us for a long time to come. It is hoped that the readers who dip into these stories find themselves drawn to the worlds they create.

Static A.D.

Ameta Bal

There are no birds. No flitting dots in the sky. No chittering from the trees outside my window. No little sparrows hopping in and out of the flowerpots in the balcony. I'm a floor up and have a good view of the street downstairs from my living room. The branches outside, motionless.

Otherwise, it's a standard summer day. It's 11:37 am. Not as hot as it will get in about an hour, but the sun is already blazing down, leaving brash streaks of golden on the road, bouncing off the bonnets of the cars parallel parked in front of the apartment and singeing the leaves on the tree.

A man, two houses down, is wiping the hood of a car, not doing a good job of cleaning anything with his sodden rag. He's only making a show of work. A woman is trying to hang up a bed sheet to dry on a clothesline in the balcony of the second-floor apartment across the road. She struggles to hoist it up, but the sheet keeps slipping. It's frustrating to watch her keep at it. I turn away from the window.

I haven't stepped out of my house in about a month. I have tea in the morning out of my blue mug, standing in front of this window every day. Other times, I make plans in my notebook. Sometimes, I try to write down my thoughts in a diary, but I'm so-so at it. There's no Tata Sky or Netflix, so I do other things. I have cleaned every nook and crevice of the house. I've been exercising; I do 50 lunges a day to make my legs stronger. I also sleep and stare out of the window a lot.

All other times, I obsess over how not to waste any food in the house so I can postpone going out, but my rations are running low. I'm going to have to step out of this apartment very soon.

I've always been an ambivert. I love people, but I don't trust them. They're beautiful on their own, unaffected, alone in their heads, being true to themselves. But put a person in front of another person and you have two monsters. Stick them all together on a ball spinning around a star and you have a blazing, spitting blob of anger, wanting and spitefulness that'll gobble up everything in its vicinity. They sold their souls many times over in the fine print, buying this iPhone and that gym membership—things that make life worth living. To buy the fun, you have to sell the air and the water and the trees. After we sold our own share of the air and water and trees, we sold the birds' and animals' shares. We received no strongly worded letter of complaint in English, so we assumed it wasn't a problem. The air and the water and the trees are only fun in words and ideas anyway. In reality, they're boring. Boredom is evil. Boredom is the villain. Without a villain, there's no story. Without a story, what's life.

The things you own, you own because of the ideas you have of yourself. If you own more things, you're still holding on to more than one idea of yourself. A person with a thousand things today is a person that keeps the hope of becoming a thousand new versions of themselves tomorrow. The Pinterest boards told us to 'Be Yourself'. Nonsense! It should have been 'Be all your selves'.

If I had lived different lives in different times, how much of myself would have remained the same? What personality traits evolve irrespective of circumstance? Could I have been a million different people in a million parallel universes? Aren't we all interchangeable really deep down? Could I not have been a pillaging, horse-riding, sword-swinging, evil-laughing Genghis Khan in one life and time, wanting this person's silver pot and that person's pretty spouse? Could I not also have been a self-effacing, floor-sweeping, bum-wiping, head-petting Mother Teresa in another life and time, giving this person a clean bedpan and that person a Catholic baptism? Do we not want to think of how I could have been a rapist in one life and a philanthropist in another? Is there no bag, shoe, wall art in the house that I own that could be proof of another me? Another me spawned by a different set of me-s who copulated on a different combination of day, month, year and place.

But if I am the me that I was always meant to be, am I this me because I've earned these lines around my eyes, the grim tilt to my mouth, the greying at the temples? Which of these body scars and this grey hair has played a part in making this specific me at 35 years of life? Or am I only made of the stories I inherit and then make up? My family's accumulated story formed the fabric on which I've patchworked my own half-assed life experiences. So many stories—big, small, vague, vivid, funny, heartbreaking; small braveries, big cowardices, odd prejudices, surprise kindnesses. My father was passionate but sacrificing, my mother, ambitious but discontented, my grandfather, gentle but stubborn, my grandmother, tenacious but overbearing. And what am I? I'm stuck in this apartment, looking out at the aunty still trying to hang up the bed sheet. And she's not always there.

A car alarm goes off in the distance, piercing the birdless silence. Judging by the sound, it's about 100 metres away, perhaps in the lane parallel to the one I'm on. I stop what I'm doing, which is burying myself deeper in my head with every passing hour, and go to the window. There's no one outside now; the street is deserted.

I decide to take stock of the food remaining in the kitchen. There's no milk or bread left, but I still have four potatoes, three onions and two packets of instant noodles.

In one corner of the kitchen shelf are two cans of unopened cat food. I think of Luna. Luna disappeared a month ago. She was in the habit of roaming the neighbourhood at night and returning in the morning, often with a present—a dry leaf, a stolen sock, even the occasional dead bird or mouse. It's been 18 days since I last saw her. I keep my ears peeled for a meow or a scratch at the door. Thinking of her lost or hurt makes my heart feel hollow, so I tell myself she hasn't returned only because she's on a neighbourhood bird extermination programme; she's the reason there are no birds out there today. It's too bad for the birds, but Luna must be stuffed and basking in a food coma high up on a wall somewhere.

Coming back to the four potatoes and three onions, I know I have to replenish my food stock. I've been postponing it. Yesterday I fell asleep after finishing my set of 50 lunges, 10 push-ups and two four-ish minute planks. I slept for three hours, and when I woke up, it was already starting to get dark. The day before, I didn't feel hungry enough to motivate myself to go out. I decided it was better to eat less anyway. Two days ago, I had a strong feeling I should stay in, in case Luna sauntered back. I don't remember what I'd told myself three or four days ago, but there's now a very pressing need to go out and get food. I don't want to be down to absolutely zero edibles before stepping out of the house. But I could do it tomorrow.

I go to my desk calendar and circle tomorrow's date with a big black marker. The last circle on the calendar is 31 days ago. Should I cross out today's date with a big black backslash? I should wait till night to do it. Live all of today first, put a backslash later. Maybe it would be a bad omen to cross out a day that hasn't yet ended. Maybe it'd mean I'd die before the day ended. Crossing out a date on the calendar is basically crossing out a day in my life. Okay, I'll live it first.

How should I live it then? I could drink that last can of beer I was saving, which now holds not just beer but a whole lot of my emotional investment. I've held on to it for so long that both the beer and the emotions are currently running on lukewarm. Lukewarm is fine. It's something, right? That's why I'm still holding onto it then.

The beer tastes good. A chilled can holds less beer than a room-temperature one anyway. Tepid beer takes longer to drink, feels fuller in the mouth, gives more bang for the buck. Lukewarm ensures you don't rush it. Lukewarm doesn't obscure details.

I pick up the sheet of newspaper lining the kitchen shelf, which holds no more beers. A two-month-old headline pops up: Riots Intensify, Troops Fire at Crowd. The world's been running too hot for too long. Opinions veering left or right. Everyone picked a side and then picked a fight. We forgot how to be still.

Remember the satiation of stillness—when our lives were as slow as the afternoon breeze, as mellow as the sunlight through the curtains and only as loud as the rustling of the leaves outside? Thoughts floated through the mind rowing boats, gently and merrily. And the lack of checkpoints or barricades meant you could go very far in the wrong direction before you realised you had to turn back and go find your friends. But they'd always be waiting for you back there.

I decide to rearrange the bookshelf while drinking my beer. Maybe I'll colour-code it this time. What if I died tomorrow along with everybody else in the entire world and my house froze in time for years and years, and then one day a person who somehow survived tomorrow's mass extinction found their way inside my perfectly arranged apartment and the first thing they saw as they walked in was this bookshelf and it was arranged in this meticulous gradation of oranges and blues and off-whites? Would that be nice? Would that be cool?

Dust everywhere but underneath it, there's a house waiting to be inhabited. Maybe they'd be the kind of person that preferred alphabetising their books before the world around them died. But in such an eventuality, would they be in a state of mind to appreciate such an order or would they be too dismal from roaming the land all by their lonesome self to note such things as a colour-coded bookcase.

Would they try to imagine me, the owner of the house and the arranger of this bookcase, and wonder about the kind of person I might have been? I hope they're a romantic.

But then, do I want to be the kind of person who colour-codes their bookshelf? Is that really me? I wouldn't want a future stranger to imagine me as someone very different from who I actually am. I should attempt the closest approximation of me. I used to be on Instagram; it can't be too hard.

I could use objects to present an absentee myself to a future visitor—a book, a photo, a quotable quote scribbled onto a Post-It. A cat or coffee isn't handy at the moment. Luna is AWOL. A testimony would have worked best. Don't we all want the kind of old, close friends that fondly summarise our personalities to strangers?

I could leave some old letters fanned out on my desk— letters written to me by friends while in school, old birthday cards, maybe some childhood photos. But that would be an outdated version of me. An origin story is pointless without a current story. I don't have any proof of the current me without the Internet—recent photos, profile feeds, Facebook likes, Twitter opinions, WhatsApp friendships.

I could just write down exactly how I view myself on some paper and tack it to the door.

I'm investing a lot of emotion in this bookcase, just as I am in every sip of this beer. It's heavy in body, with nostalgic undertones and a nice emotional finish. I also sense a slight lingering bitterness for what's not there.

The thing about investing emotion is if we don't put value on this nugget and that experience, we're lost.

We forgot how to feel the good feelings, and then we chose to forget that we forgot. All that remained was rage. Rage to your right and then the rage to your left. But the centre was left hollow. And that's when it came—the end of the world.

The electricity is gone, the water's stopped. Life, as we know it, has ended. It was on the TV and the Internet— the videos and photos of the first phase of mysterious mass deaths, the second phase of rioting and total societal breakdown and then the deluge of isolated experiences and theories from solitary survivors—all before our electronic gadgets went on the blink.

I've been here for 31 days, only with myself. For 31 days, I haven't pressed a play, like or send button. I haven't typed or heard any words, except the ones in my head. There are no buttons left to press.

It may be time.

I crush the empty can and place it on the table beside the sofa. There's a folded sheet on my bed that I tuck under my armpit. My sneakers are lying next to the main door. I slip my feet into them and put my hand on the door handle. Tomorrow will be no different than today.

I undo the double lock on the door and twist the handle. The stairway outside is darker than the apartment, so I push the door wide open to let the late afternoon light from the apartment window into the staircase. It's one flight of stairs down. I walk past the closed door of the empty ground-floor house. The landlord had neither lived there nor ever rented it out. The locked door is a familiar sight. I open the main door that feeds the stairwell, and daylight streams in. It hurts my eyes a little.

I walk through the driveway and push open the tall gates. They creak only a little, like an IMAX action movie scene. Is there another me in one of these houses somewhere who heard that?

The colony road is as it generally was at this time of the day, quieter than usual. What's missing is the sound of faraway traffic. There are cars parked on both sides of the road in either direction. I turn left and walk a little way till the road hits another perpendicular road. This, too, is flanked by houses on both sides, although bigger ones. This one has tall trees on the boundary walls obstructing the view of the houses from the road. Some of these gates have locks on them. I take another left and start walking in the middle of the road. I can see the corner of the park up ahead and the milk booth with its shutters down.

Once I reach the T-point, I pull the sheet out from under my arm and spread it open in the middle of the crossing. I lie down with my hands tucked under my head and look up at the sky through the arching branches. It's still blue. The sun is now hiding behind the Gulmohar at the end of the road, and a gentle breeze sneaks in. The leaves of the Amaltas in its yellow summer glory start to rustle. Is this enough?

Time passes, either in minutes or in hours. If I let it go, there's no one keeping it.

I let it go, all of it. Was it even mine to let go? It was all snatched. But I agree to return it now, like a long overdue library book, which at first you needed, then you outgrew, but forgot to return, and in the end, it was just too late.

The sun slips away, and as the shadows glide past me, I gradually become aware of the direction to my house. I try to stay still, but the air around me feels heavier. Raising myself up on my elbows, I look at the milk-booth shutters, still down, then at the Gulmohar tree, now a dull ochre instead of a light yellow. This doesn't feel right anymore. I turn my head to look in the direction I came. Something moves in the distance, but very close to the treeline.

Luna? I jump up. My chest feels tight. Did Luna find me? I should have come out sooner to look for her.

I gather up my sheet and squint in the direction of the movement. It's not a cat. A figure is limping unhurriedly towards me. Its arms hang straight down its sides, one longer than the other. I take a step back. Am I not alone?

I face the approaching figure and wait. At about 15 metres, I see it, just as it sees me. It's a man with dead eyes. In all this time with myself I must have subdued the images I'd seen on my Twitter feed. Images of undead people feeding on the other undead. Maybe it was the other way round. Maybe my brain short-circuited, and I didn't know which way was dead and which way alive.

I remember looking at this man repeating a motion hardwired into a brain from routine. A sodden rag, threadbare from being rubbed on a car hood, dangles from his hand. My feet feel stuck to the ground, but his find purpose.

He comes at me, the only way he knows how to come at another—with rage.

A Tale of Disconnect

Anila SK

District Court Number 7 in Hulfsdorp, a busy suburb of Colombo, is where men dispose what God had once proposed. People come here to accept decisions contrary to the dreams they had once cherished. For some, it was redemption, for others, liberation fraught with pain and agony. Margi had never imagined being a plaintiff at the witness stand in a courtroom, where there was an inscription in a language she could not read—Sinhalese.

Each tick of the grandfather clock behind the judge's seat in the crowded courtroom tugged at her heart until her heartbeat paced faster than the rhythmic ticks.

'The proceedings have to be in English, as my client does not speak Sinhalese,' her lawyer announced.

The judge looked at the plaintiff, Margi, dressed in a plain white sari with a light green border. An unprecedented calmness and a chilling resolve dominated her presence, although her most-dreaded moments were coming live.

'So, you are from Kerala, India?' the lawyer began.

'Yes.'

'You were happy at the initial stages of your marriage?'

'Yes.'

'Then your husband's irrational and inconsiderate behaviour led to arguments and disagreements?'

'Yes.'

Margi paused each time before she answered, and the pauses became longer each time. She stammered first, then answered in monosyllables. She was trying to categorically dismiss a dysfunctional marriage despite the overpowering palpitation she experienced at that moment.

The judge's eyes hardly shifted away from her. The eerily quiet courtroom was filled with long gasps of several other men and women, waiting their turn. The gasps reflected disquietude. Or relief. Or memories. Or just nothing.

Margi and her ex-husband, declared so a few moments ago, walked parallel out of the courtroom. He walked along the corridor right above her, while she trampled the lawn. They did not plan to walk parallel. It just so happened.

'Buha kutcha macha,' A weird voice splintered through. A differently abled boy was playing with his nanny on the same lawn. Margi walked towards him as if in a trance. He was boisterous and playful, making odd sounds and bouncing in circles.

'Do not take him seriously, he speaks a language no one understands,' the knackered nanny told Margi.

'Does he stammer?' Margi was pensive.

'Yes, often,' the unemotional nanny murmured.

They were waiting for the boy's mother, whose case was being heard in the same courtroom.

Margi could hear his undecipherable lingo while walking out of the morbid court premises, leaving a decade of marriage behind her to a city streaming with automobiles.

The late monsoon rains splattered heavily as if the gods had grown angry. Or were they crying?

It was a moment of pondering.

Her feet felt the muddy earth. A few paper boats came floating and touched her muddy feet. And stopped.

We did not own anything then, yet we felt as if we were part of a large world, where everything good existed. The world looked real until reality started changing hues. Even gods looked like real people.

Narayanan, please sit beside me, to write our story...

Three decades ago, in the early eighties, the TATA school bus was cheering past the other school taxis. Who will win the morning race? The jubilant children inside would cheer the 'Driver Uncles' to win over others. The uncles would speed within reasonable limits. Jeez! The mornings used to start on a high note of excitement for many schoolgoers in the city of Trivandrum, a coastal town in Kerala. Sundays remained eerily quiet and deserted.

Narayanan, always impeccably dressed in his navy-blue shorts and white shirt, sported a snooty look. The piercing peep through the thick black glasses, with his head slightly tilted down, made him look nerdy, lost to the world. A square-shaped bottle of water was a permanent fixture around his neck. He waited for his mighty school bus to invade the roads, pick him up grandly and relegate the black-and-white taxis to second-class automobiles. From his permanent window seat of the school bus, he observed the world from a plane higher than the rest. The one and only black Morris Minor car that sped fast, whose bonnet resembled an adult's mouth puffed with unchewable half-boiled rice, looked to him as if it were trying to explain the meaning of its meagre existence.

If any taxi sped past Narayanan's vigilant eyes, he would catapult a small stone, aiming at the rim of the rear tire. Plonk! No harm. In return, Narayanan was liberally sprayed with water, and occasionally with lime juice, by the children inside the taxis, who used to anticipate his antics. Before he could pelt more stones, the taxi would disappear in a flash.

Narayanan would stay in anticipation of his next-best opportunity to pelt. In the evenings, near the Carmel Convent, the school pickups congregated under a huge sapodilla tree, which bore countless fruits almost all year round. Any noise around the tree was met with serious warnings by the sentry, who was never enthused by the children's antics.

'You can't hang around here and pelt stones at the fruits! Diminutive rascals!'

He spat the blood-red juice of the betel leaves while swaying his cane. Children ran for shelter behind the vehicles, only to reappear when the sentry went in.

Narayanan was the first to run towards the sapodilla tree until others finished school.

While others returned in their mud-smeared shirts, with a dangling shoe lace, enjoying the blissful freedom after school, Narayanan still had his white shirt unsmeared, tucked over his shorts, worn slightly above his protruding belly. He was impeccable.

Narayanan then led the customary Collector's Show under the sapodilla tree, usually with less opposition or none at all. He displayed the day's loot with the precision of a bookkeeper, especially to his arch-rival Margi, who travelled in the KLV 8275 black-and-white Ambassador taxi that carried twice more children than it could accommodate.

'Now you show yours,' he said to Margi, spreading his God Cards.

'You thought I did not have any?' Margi spread out the tarot-card-sized pictures of goddesses and gods, made familiar through illustrated books that set childhood imagination wild. Gods could do everything like normal people, sometimes a lot more that put human beings to shame.

Christ's face was always solemn. Hindu gods were far too many and colourful. But it did not quite matter. After all, they were all gods.

'Why does the Christ always have a beard?' Margi was curious.

Narayanan peeped through his thick glasses. With an academic precision, he blurted out, 'Maybe he liked it very much and did not want to shave.'

'Hm,' Margi was not convinced.

Each card had a story behind, usually scrupulously long and occasionally short.

Narayanan's favourite was a slice from the epic Ramayana, where the monkey god, Hanuman, carried a huge mountain on his finger tip. A monkey carried a mountain! That too on his finger tip! No questions were asked. A monkey can also be a god, and gods could carry mountains. It was well accepted.

Margi flaunted a new card. Narayanan was trying to hide his disappointment at her new acquisition.

'Hmm. You really don't know me. I am God Incarnate. I can exhume godly powers and mince you into pieces, if I wish.' Margi looked stubborn.

'You idiot. Look at you! Girls should behave better.'

Both paused for a second to get the better of each other and were lost for words.

'Children, get into your vehicles, we are about to leave,' the driver's assistant announced.

Margi felt a sudden wetness on her back. There was Narayanan, ballistic, spraying water at her from the very same water bottle he always had around his neck.

'Hmm, wait until I catch you, you potbellied...' she made a face.

Name-calling like this was considered natural in the early eighties. Best friends would fight like this. The world did not see this as disrespect or discrimination. Parents left their children to their natural tendencies of name-calling. Any wound was just dealt with a dash of Dettol in lukewarm water. If a fall happened in school, the choice was to remain brave to avoid that brown-coloured first-aid liquid that sent hot tears down the cheek or go home and face the Dettol dash, spiced with warnings by a parent. Sympathy was not heard of.

Immaculately, the pain vanished the next day. In a week, all that remained was a scab, which was purposely tugged to bleed further. A week later, just a scar remained—unlike the scars that were to leave lifetime blemishes, decades after.

Margi truly believed that she was God Incarnate. The problem, she thought, was with the rest of the world that did not believe in the secret powers she possessed. She visualised levitating in her celestial aura, displaying her hidden powers, like gods in the myriad stories she had read. Her fantasies were as colourful as the sequins and stones she collected from artificial jewellery, which she counted and recounted at the crack of mornings. Then she wrapped them with a thin pink paper, knotted with a piece of cloth and stacked away secretly.

'Do you know I want to be a gem merchant when I grow up?' she wanted to sound rich and expensive.

'Gem? Do you even know what it means, girl?' Narayanan was sarcastic.

Margi handed out a sparkling pink stone proudly. Narayanan was flabbergasted. His eyes started to roll behind those thick glasses. He looked at Margi with admiration and disbelief.

Margi ran away, fully knowing that Narayanan had fallen for her secret riches. That day, Sanjay, a newcomer, joined Narayanan's school bus. Slightly taller than others, he, too, got down to witness the day's loot of Margi and Narayanan.

'I got five today,' Narayanan was boastful.

Margi's face fell as she had only one new card. Narayanan was on a winning mode.

'You told me yesterday that you are a goddess. So, show your powers now.'

'Goddess?' the newcomer exclaimed. 'You liar. No one can be a god or goddess. They are all in the skies, not on earth.'

Margi felt that she was losing face to Sanjay.

'No, I do have special powers,' she maintained her position.

'Show, show!' Sanjay demanded.

Margi ran towards the sapodilla tree and tried to fight her tears. Sanjay followed her and pulled at her shirt sleeve. Margi gently pushed him away. He returned the act with more force, and Margi fell.

Narayanan descended from nowhere and furiously charged towards them.

'She has special powers, I have seen them,' he exhorted.

'Let us go back,' Narayanan held Margi's hand and walked away silently.

Margi affectionately gifted him her new God Card before boarding the school taxi.

He took it, smiling.

The next morning turned out to be different.

'Get off the road, my child,' a desperate mother was pleading with her son who had decided to sit in the middle of the road, stopping the traffic. He was an oversized child. A fellow motorist got down from his car and pleaded with the boy. The boy yelled louder.

The man reluctantly dragged him towards the gate of the 'Deaf and Dumb' school, next to Margi's.

The boy was still keening, and his mother in tears. Margi's taxi also queued up due to this commotion. While escorted by the taxi driver towards her school gate, she kept looking back at the boy being dragged.

'What are you looking at? Get back to your classrooms,' came a bombardment from a senior teacher at Margi's school.

The morning school bell rang, and Margi rushed to her class. She hurriedly spread out the pack of God Cards. Many gods looked up at her. Why did you make children who are different from me, who sit in the middle of the roads and make their mothers cry, who refuse to walk on their own, whose faces are big and eyes are small?

No god answered.

Margi kept waiting for someone who would give her a believable answer.

No one did.

The year passed quickly. Margi and friends earned a few brash bruises on their knees and elbows. Margi moved to fifth standard, and Narayanan remained in standard three for the third consecutive year in the school for 'Deaf and Dumb'.

'Is he deaf and dumb, Amma?' she asked her mother.

'Yes.'

'But he does everything like me. Only he speaks a bit differently.'

'Haven't you noticed? He looks different too.'

'Oh, does he?'

'He was just a bit bigger than others. He spilled water on me. Called me names. Threw stones and walked fast. Protected me from bullies. Of course, he spoke differently. Would this make him different? How? I did too...'

It was when Margi was in the upper kindergarten, all the children were put to sleep in the afternoon by Tara, their loving class teacher.

'Margi, close your eyes, don't fool me.'

Margi got caught. She tried to peep through the corner of her eyes.

'Aunty, K...K...Kthipa is not giving me space.'

'Who? Kripa?'

'Yes, K...K...Kthipa.'

Margi had tried to emulate Kripa the first day in montessori, but the effort was fruitless.

Kripa had feigned hunger and sprinted out of the class crying loud, uttering a language Margi did not know that time—Tamil. '*Appa, pasikkithee!*' (Papa, I am hungry!) Kripa was tenderly brought back by Tara teacher.

The same Kripa was not giving her space now. To sleep.

'R' was a sound, others told Margi, she could not utter. She paused long between words and struggled to get the first sound of a word out. Anyhow, she did not know the difference, except that it was a 'deficiency' all spoke about. She made instant verses and completed the lyrics of the poems she heard in her own version. But no 'r' surfaced in any of them, instead 'th' did.

'Sweet pthetty Sita, wheye aa yoe fthom? Wht is yoe name?' Sita, her white doll, like all other inanimate things, was also a living being for her.

The words assigned to things by the world were dissimilar to what she assumed them to be.

'This is a spoon, say Margi,' her mother was trying to teach her.

'This is a poond.'

'A poond?'

'Yes.'

A week later.

'Now try saying spoon.'

'A thoomb.' Margi sat motionless.

'Aiyo, this is a spoon, sweetheart.'

'A thoomb.'

Her mother never resumed classes again.

'Margi, this is a ribbon, say, ribbon,' Manikkutty, her elder sister, took on the responsibility.

'This is a daval.'

'What?'

'A daval… No, dommam.'

'Daval, dommam, what next? She will never come right Amma!' Cried her sister.

Margi did not know what desperation at failed attempts could mean. Her world was fresh and disconnected from the rest.

And, that afternoon, she tried to hoodwink Tara teacher and got caught for not sleeping after lunch.

'Kripa, move,' Margi said.

KRipa—that 'R'! She could not believe that 'r' sound came from her larynx!

'KRripa, KRipa, KRipa,' she screamed non-stop, unbelievingly.

'What happened, Margi?' Tara aunty worriedly rushed towards her.

'Aunty, that 'R' came. I could say, K...KRipa. See, 'K...KRipa!' Her eyes were gleaming. I am not MaTHgi any more... MaRgi, I am!'

Margi did not know what it meant to 'lisp' or 'stammer.' But she knew 'they were deficiencies' she overcame that day.

That evening, she celebrated the discovery of 'R' in her life and the suddenness of the first sound of any word, by sliding on the cement slope in school and getting her baby ass scraped.

'I can say KRipa...KRipa...' she excitedly ran to her sister, who came to pick her up.

Manikkutty, welling up with tears, tightly embraced the little brat who was busy showing her scraped ass.

'Good girl! So, no more crying inside the bus from today. Okay? I am ashamed of your crying.'

True, Margi gave her teenage sister hell inside a crowded bus by wailing loud, until their parents decided to send her in a taxi. She hated crowds, always.

There was a strong disconnect between what Margi thought was true and saw, and what others said about them. Gods in the epics were supposed to know all answers. But even they did not know some or maybe refused to answer. Narayanan and Margi were different, but Margi never knew the difference when they were together. Did he?

'I kept giving different names for things. Had long pauses between words and struggled to say words. They called it a lisp and a stammer. Narayanan did not have these deficiencies. Yet, he could only go to a 'Deaf and Dumb' school. Why?' she asked her good friend, God.

No god answered her. Not that day. Not any other day.

A time came when the once-unanswered questions removed their shroud and revealed themselves bare, shamelessly stark naked. Reality became a malignancy that grew fast, beyond recognition. They called it growing up. Once that happened, life never remained the same again.

Stillness of nights paved way for the streaming beams, only to fade into darkness again.

Only the rains were relentless. The gods were still silent, as if they wanted no more questions about her past. A new world waited for her, someone whispered. She turned around to see who it was.

Pandemonium

Anjali Doney

Jessie woke up to the bristle of her cat's tail against her feet. 'Shunky!' She protested groggily. Through half-open eyes, Jessie saw a dead rat dangling from Shunky's mouth.

'Big kill last night, eh?' she said. 'Now please get rid of it before Ammachi sees you.'

Jessie had found Shunky years ago—a grey kitten hiding on her window sill from a monsoon storm. She considered herself an ideal cat keeper. She let Shunky hunt during the night and roam freely during the day, coming home for food and naps. She didn't pamper her too much but treated her to the occasional back rub. They understood each other's moods, sounds and body language.

From under the blanket, Jessie reached for the tape recorder on the nightstand and pressed the play button. ABBA's *Voulez-Vous* blasted through the speakers. The album had come out two years ago, in 1979, but had only recently reached the shores of the small city of Cochin and was now all the rage. Jessie finally felt awake. Everyone in the house, too, knew she was awake.

She made her way to the kitchen to fix a lemon and honey face mask. A cup of hot milk was set aside for her. Her mother was frantically making tea for everyone else, pouring it back and forth between two aluminium mugs to form a generous layer of froth. Jessie loved tea, but milk was good for the skin. She had read that goat's milk was even better.

'Ammachi, can we get goat's milk?' she asked.

'Who do you think you are? Cleopatra?' Came the sharp response. That was Jessie's cue to get out of her mother's hair.

Jessie knocked at her younger brother's door.

'Wardrobe crisis today also?' he asked, yawning. ABBA was playing in his room as well.

James was sweet for a 14 year-old. Whenever Jessie didn't feel like wearing any of her own clothes, he let her raid his almirah. Her eyes fell on a white linen shirt with bold blue stripes that would pair perfectly with her navy-blue bell-bottoms.

His shirts fit her well, except they were too long. So, she tied the bottom ends into a fashionable knot in the front. To finish the look, she plaited her thick, curly hair in two braids and climbed into a pair of white platform shoes. She opened her big, black umbrella and left for the bus stop.

'Looks like someone escaped from jail today,' the bus conductor said to no one in particular as she got on the bus.

A comment on her striped shirt and the fact that her stop was Qasba Police Station. She pursed her lips to keep from laughing, but he saw a corner of her mouth go up and was satisfied.

Jessie saw her friend Usha in the front and made her way there, hanging onto the railing above, as the bus sped ahead.

'See, Jess, my mother let me wear her saree today,' Usha said, stumbling, as she eagerly held up the loose end of the saree.

'It's lovely!' Jessie beamed, 'I'm sure your Thaadikaaran will love it.'

Usha blushed.

Thaadikaaran (or beard-man) was their nickname for a scrawny, bearded chap they saw regularly on their way to college, with whom Usha made intense eye contact. He was the portrait of a struggling artist, complete with faded kurta, jute bag and long hair. Neither party had the gall to take things further, afraid of shattering the illusion they had built up over weeks. Instead, the girls tried to guess what his life must be like and his actual name.

Usha was the U in DANJERUS.

Jessie had coined the acronym for their extended group of friends using their initials—Diane, Asha, Nafisa, Jessie, Esther, Renuka, Usha and Shiela. They were all in degree first year, having finished the two years of pre-degree at the same college. Of the lot, Usha and Renuka were the closest to her.

Renuka was waiting for them under the tree outside the Economics Department. It was a large tamarind tree surrounded by a raised stone platform, on which students lounged between classes, sheltered from the scorching sun.

St. Teresa's was an all-women's college run by nuns. Adjacent to it was Maharaja's College, the epicentre of Cochin's student politics, and further down the road was Law College, where all the eligible bachelors went.

The first period was political science by Sister Rosetta. Jessie and the DANJERUS girls occupied the last two rows. They tried to stay awake through the hour. Sister Rosetta cleared her throat.

'Has anyone brought anything for the annual magazine?' she asked. 'The deadline is approaching.'

A girl in the front row promptly got up and gave the teacher a sheet of paper.

'Didn't Priya submit something yesterday as well?' Diane asked her friends in genuine amazement.

'Aiyyo! Without this Priya, there would be no college magazine,' Nafisa said much louder than she meant to. All the girls in the back giggled.

'Silence!' thundered Sister Rosetta. 'Jessie, stand up.'

Jessie stood up, cursing her luck for sitting right behind Nafisa.

'Please share the joke with the class,' continued Sister Rosetta, 'none of us in the front could hear it.'

'I didn't say anything, Sister,' said Jessie.

'Then who did?' she demanded.

Jessie kept mum.

'Since you're so smart,' said Sister Rosetta, 'I want to see an entry from you for the magazine.'

After the class, Nafisa apologised to Jessie for getting her into trouble.

'Should I write the magazine entry for you?' Nafisa offered with a big grin, 'Maybe an essay?'

'No thanks!' Jessie said, 'I'd like to keep my reputation intact.'

Nafisa laughed. She was kidding, of course. Nafisa's spelling was known to be so terrible that her friends couldn't fathom how she had passed school.

'Or, you know, I could do a simple painting for you, if you want,' she suggested in more seriousness. That wasn't a bad idea, Jessie thought.

Usha and Renuka had their second hour free, so Jessie skipped hers too and joined them at their usual juice shop. It was right behind their college, in Convent Junction, the most happening spot in the city where all the young people congregated and mingled.

'One grape juice, one cold coffee, one mango shake!' the shopkeeper called to the back as soon as he saw the girls. He knew his regular patrons' orders by heart.

They sat down at the corner table with a view of the cigarette shop across the narrow lane, a row of motorcycles alongside it. Young men loitered about, smoking cigarettes or chewing gum. Suddenly, everybody turned their heads in unison to a group of seniors walking out from the college back gate. The final-year girls moved like a force, laughing like there was no care in the world, swaying their hips, the ends of their tightly draped sarees blowing in the wind. 'Like lionesses,' observed Jessie. Usha looked at her own saree—how come hers was not blowing like theirs?

A motorcycle roared to a stop, catching Jessie's attention. It was a military green Yezdi. The number plate was familiar to her. Heck, the specific hum of the vehicle was familiar to her. She was not a motorcycle enthusiast. She had just developed a keen interest in its owner.

The strapping fellow parked the bike and stepped off it in one smooth motion, barely glancing at the girls around. He ran his hands through his messy hair. He was tall and had a permanent five o'clock shadow on his gaunt face. Being 22 gave him an aura of wisdom among the present crowd of teenagers and college students.

The girls had more intel on him than on Thaadikaaran. His name was Asif. He had dropped out from Maharaja's the year before. He had to be from a big business family to afford the motorcycle. What he did for a living, or in general, was a mystery.

Jessie wasn't sure if he walked slower than everyone else or if time just seemed to slow down when he was around. He strode to the cigarette vendor; he never walked, he only strode. The way everyone nodded to him was reminiscent of a hat tip.

One of the seniors, Lubeena, stopped to chat with him. She was breathtaking, clad in a red chiffon saree, her skin like ivory, her hair tied in a low bun. A Cleopatra! She was the head of the Students' Cultural Union. When he gave her a piece of orange candy, Jessie's insides ached.

'You know what,' she said getting up, 'I'm going to write him a letter.'

'Don't you have anything better to do?' Renuka asked flatly.

'It's just that I can't contain these feelings, Renu,' she tried to explain.

'Write to him, Jess,' Usha encouraged. 'Better get it off your chest.'

'You do realise he must be getting love notes every single day?' Renuka reasoned.

'You think so?' Jessie asked. Renuka could be right, she reckoned, but she felt a strong cosmic connection with Asif that deserved to be given a chance.

She took in one last eyeful of him to tap into those sentiments when drafting the letter, and the girls parted ways. Renuka and Usha back to college, and Jessie to the lending library on the next street.

The library owner, Shenoy, was something of a mentor to Jessie and other bookworms like her. He gave them book recommendations based on their taste and occasionally some unsolicited life advice.

'Shenoy Sir, can I borrow these today?' Jessie asked, handing him a piece of paper.

'Didn't you read these last month already?' Shenoy asked her curiously.

'Yes, but I need to go through some parts again,' she explained. 'For a college project,' she added.

He looked at her with suspicion. 'Alright, but you know my rules, no underlining words.'

Whenever Jessie came across a word that she loved, she would jot it down in the back of her diary. She had collected a long catalogue of words, but to be sure she used them in the right way in her letter, she planned to refer to these novels.

She found an empty classroom, tore out a page of ruled paper from her notebook and started writing. The opening line was the most difficult. She had to make an impact from the get-go. She wrote and rewrote it.

To the boy with dishevelled hair and the rugged motorcycle.

No. He'd like it more if she called him a man. And maybe *windswept* was a better word.

To the man with windswept hair and the rugged motorcycle. I have my qualms about writing this letter, but I cannot rest if I don't.

Just then, the English teacher poked her head in the door.

'What happened, Jessie?' she asked in faux concern. 'Are you actually studying or writing imposition?'

'Studying, Miss,' answered Jessie with a polite smile specially reserved for teachers.

She spent the rest of the morning penning the letter, tempering it with words and phrases she relished. It was a page long. After she finished, she folded the piece of paper neatly and put it in her pocket. She went to meet her friends, who she knew would be under the department tree having their lunch.

'Where have you been?' Renuka asked.

'Writing a letter is an art and takes time,' Jessie said dramatically, helping herself to a spoonful of lemon rice from Usha's tiffin box. 'Can we go give it to him now before I change my mind?'

The girls went back to Convent Junction to look for him. The place was much more crowded now that it was the middle of the lunch hour.

'How can I give it to him in front of all these people?' she said. Her forehead dampened.

'Well, there he is,' Usha spotted him crouched down behind his motorcycle a short distance away from the cigarette shop. He was fixing the brake wires on the back wheel.

It was a now-or-never moment. Jessie drew up a plan of action.

The girls first went to the cigarette shop on the pretext of buying orange candy. Then they walked past him as if they were heading to the stationery store. Jessie stopped by the motorcycle, while her friends slowed down a few steps ahead. When he looked up, she stuck the note in the motorcycle's seat and hurried on as fast as her platform heels could carry her. She caught up with the girls, and they disappeared down the library lane.

'Did he say anything?' Usha asked when they were safely out of sight.

'I don't think so,' Jessie replied. 'Did you see his face?'

'No, why? What was his face like?' asked Usha.

'I don't know,' Jessie said, 'I went blank.'

Jessie couldn't fall asleep that night. Shunky sensed her restlessness and curled up next to her in bed.

In the morning, her stomach was in a knot. Part of her wanted to hide in her bedroom forever and part of her burned to see him again. She fantasised about what he might say and rehearsed her responses.

She daydreamed through macroeconomic theory in the first period. Then there was a sociology test she had completely forgotten about in the second. Free in the third period, with Renuka and Usha stuck in history class, she decided to go on a little recce of her own.

From her bag, she took out the five novels she had borrowed and carried them in her arms so it would look like she was going to the library. She walked at a brisk, matter-of-fact pace. As she approached the juice shop, she wanted to slow down and take a look around, but her feet refused to stop and her head refused to move.

'Hey!' a deep voice called from the line of motorcycles to her right.

Jessie froze. She willed her body to turn. Asif was coming towards her.

'Jessie, right?' he asked, 'Can I see that book?'

He pointed to the top of the pile. She gave it to him.

'I read your note,' he said, flipping through the book slowly, 'You write really well.'

Jessie's heart somersaulted to her mouth.

'In fact,' he spoke slowly with a smile, 'I think you like words more than you like any guy.'

Jessie's face turned a pomegranate pink.

'I didn't even understand some of them. What does *pandemonium* mean?' he asked.

'It means madness and,' she swallowed some air, 'and chaos.'

'Nice,' he said as if he meant it. 'Do you write a lot?'

She shook her head. 'Not really. Just in my diary sometimes.'

'You know Lubeena?' he continued, 'She said they were looking for an editor for the college magazine.'

'Oh no, no, no!' Jessie cried out, suddenly finding her voice. 'Please! You cannot tell her about this!'

'I won't if you won't,' he said with a chuckle. He put the chit she had given him in the book and gave it back to her. 'Maybe it's best if you hold on to this.'

She nodded.

'Friends?' he asked.

She gathered the courage to lift her head and look him in the eye. She had never seen his face this close. His eyes were kind. Her stomach sank.

'Yeah sure,' she said with as much nonchalance as she could muster.

Once she turned the corner, Jessie dumped the books in her bag and caught the next bus home. She stuck her face to the window, letting the wind blow the barrage of emotions away. How could she have been foolish enough to believe her big, fancy words could match the beauty and brains of Lubeena? To hell with *pandemonium*.

Back home, she helped her mother wash clothes and hang them out to dry. She talked to James about the Beatles, and John Lennon's death—their pet topic of discussion. She gave Shunky the leftover fish from dinner and watched her lick the plate clean. Still, she couldn't stop picturing Asif and Lubeena laughing at her letter over heaps of orange candy. She scribbled an angry poem on the futility of existence.

In college the next day, she gave Renuka and Usha an elaborate re-enactment of the incident, including the way he walked and his eyebrow movement, and more quietly, about Lubeena.

'It could have gone much worse,' consoled Renuka.

'At least, you're not strangers now,' chimed in Usha.

'I wish we were,' said Jessie.

As promised, Nafisa brought a painting of a waterfall for the magazine, but Jessie went out on a limb and submitted her existential poem instead. She convinced Nafisa to hand in her artwork too. Sister Rosetta was thrilled to have the backbenchers defy her expectations of them.

Jessie avoided Convent Junction for three days, after which the need for cold drinks and social interactions surpassed feelings of embarrassment. Guarded by her circle of friends, she made it to the juice shop. Halfway through her drink, she felt Renuka nudging her. She looked up to see Asif and Lubeena walking in. Before she could duck under the table, he saw her.

'Lubu, this is Jessie,' Asif said in his baritone.

'Hi,' said Lubeena, flashing her dimples, 'my brother says you write really well.'

'Brother!' Jessie blurted out, 'He's your brother?'

'Yes, big brother,' Lubeena said, 'Hard to believe, no?'

'Yeah!' Jessie exclaimed, grinning from ear to ear.

'You must write for our magazine,' Lubeena insisted.

'I have,' Jessie replied proudly, 'and I'm working on more.' She wasn't, but how hard could it be?

Jessie and Asif became friends over time, the kind who say *What's up?* and *How was the weekend?* There was a skip in her step again.

Renuka still kept a watchful eye on her. Jessie, in turn, looked out for Usha, particularly on the bus. Usha continued to exchange glances with Thaadikaaran. They never found out his name.

Terms and Conditions
Camilla Chester

It was the only birthday card Laura hadn't yet opened. Who was she kidding? It was the only card she had been given, well, from work at least. It had been waiting for her when she arrived at her desk. It sat there still, ridiculously conspicuous against the brown wallet file of Mrs Emmersley, the lonely client who talked endlessly. Insurance meant everything was recorded in detail; Mrs Emmersley's file had, therefore, become as fat as Bulgy Brian.

Perhaps the card was from him? She hoped not. Laura peeped spy-like over the top of her computer monitor. Brian caught her eye, mid crisp stuff, grinned and put up a greasy thumb.

'Having a good one?'

Laura half-smiled. 'Rather not be at work for my birthday, but yeah, I guess. Thanks.' She cringed at herself. What had become of her life? Of her dreams? Thirty-six, single and stuck in a crappy job shifting papers from one side of her desk to another. Pointless.

She eyed the shiny envelope. It was decorated with fluorescent swirls so lurid it made her squint. There was a break in calls, so she opened it neatly, in one scissor-slice.

The front of the card read in embossed, spongy, multi-coloured letters: CONGRATULATIONS! YOUR WISHES HAVE BEEN GRANTED. Laura opened the card expecting it to house some age-related pun that would make her groan and feel even worse about herself, but instead the inside of the card was filled with minuscule writing. Reams of it, all laid out in endless bullet points, exactly like an insurance policy document. The letters were way too small to read. She couldn't make head nor tail of it. She flipped the card over, but the back was just the same swirly design as the front.

She felt around inside the envelope, but it was empty. She was wondering if she had some kind of magnifying lens that she could use to read the tiny words when her phone lit up. Already wearing her headset, she took the call.

'Thank you for calling Port Holland. You're speaking to Laura. How can I help?'

'Laura Pimpleback?'

Laura waited for the inevitable joke about her horrible surname. She'd expected to be married by now and have left it long behind. The caller was silent, so Laura said, 'Yes?'

'Hi. This is Aaliyah—on reception downstairs?'

'Oh right, sorry. I hadn't realised it was an internal call.' Why was she always sorry?

'Listen, I think you better come down. There's a delivery for you, sort of unusual.'

The whole way down, Laura was imagining all kinds of possible boring scenarios, but she did not expect to be greeted by a small man in an elf-costume with a wide grin.

Aaliyah was on another call. She pulled a face at Laura and shrugged.

'Laura!' said the elf-man, like they went way back. 'Happy birthday and congratulations to you. Your first wish is here.'

'My what?'

The man reached deep into the right pocket of his green felt shorts and pulled out a piece of paper that had been folded up into a small, neat square. 'Says it right here, November 22nd on a chicken wishbone, pulled with brother, Nigel. Aged 11. Lifetime supply of sweets.' The elf-man looked up from the paper and grinned at her. 'Where do you want them?'

'Wait. What? Where do I? What are you talking about?'

'You are Laura Pimpleback of 33, Granville Avenue, right?'

'Granville Ave...I haven't lived at that address since I was 18,' said Laura.

'Ah, but you did live there when you made the wish. Am I right or am I right?'

'Wish?' What was this funny little elf-man going on about? Laura looked back at the receptionist, but she was no help.

'Yes, the wish you made when you beat your brother and got the bone, remember?'

'I can't remember every wish I might or might not have made when I was 11 years old,' said Laura, unable to believe she was being pulled into this ridiculous prank.

'Lucky you won't have to then, isn't it?'

Laura stared at him blankly.

'It's all clearly stipulated in the terms and conditions,' the elf-man explained in a slightly less jovial tone. 'One wish is selected from each year until your 15th birthday. Five wishes in total. So, back to my first question. Where do you want the sweets?'

The man nodded his elf hat towards the large glass doors at the front of the office reception. A team of UPS delivery staff were busy stacking boxes up in the lobby.

'You can't leave those there,' Aaliyah said, unplugging the lead of her headset and making her way round the reception desk. 'It's a health and safety infringement.'

Laura followed her and began reading the labels on the boxes: Sherbet Dib-Dabs x 150, Mixed Liquorice All-sorts x 150, 1000 grams Sherbet Pips.

'I don't even like sweets any more,' she said. 'This has to be some kind of wind-up.'

The boxes kept on coming. Never-ending Cola-Cubes and Sherbet Lemons, Honey-comb Crunch and Watermelon Bon-Bons.

'Can't you deliver them to an children's charity or something?' Laura asked, scratching at the back of her neck.

'If that's what you want,' he said and sadly folded up the paper again.

'I think it's best,' Laura said, relieved. 'I do want to keep my teeth after all.'

The elf-man snorted. 'Back in the van,' he instructed the delivery staff, 'we have a rejector.'

'Apart from this one,' said Laura in a rush. She picked up the box on the top that was labelled 'Crumbly Fudge in 250g packets' and tucked it under her arm.

Later, Laura's brother, Nigel, came over to the flat with a bottle of red wine for her birthday. He'd stayed and was helping her to drink it. Surprisingly, it complemented the fudge quite well.

'He was wearing an elf costume?'

Laura nodded. 'I kept looking around for hidden cameras.' She took a good slug of wine. 'You didn't have anything to do with it, did you?'

'Nope,' Nigel said. 'Have any other wishes come true?'

'I've been trying to remember what wishes I made.' Laura could remember very well the wishes she made aged 15. Surely nothing to do with Robin Godiva would come true, would it? She cringed and tingled simultaneously at the thought.

Nigel shifted round to face her. 'I remember something,' he said as he put his elbow onto the table and opened his hand towards her, 'I know that you definitely wished to beat me.'

Laura smiled. It was true, she had often wished to be stronger than her big brother and beat him in an arm wrestle. He always won. It was totally infuriating, especially when he gloated afterwards. Nigel flexed his bicep and winked at her. Laura took up the challenge and her hand grabbed his.

'Are you sure you want to do this?' Nigel said, and his eyebrow did that patronising half-lift. Laura tightened her jaw in response.

'Okay, but don't say I didn't warn you. Three, two, one, go.'

It was effortless, as if Nigel's muscles were nothing but butter, and his hand instantly hit the table so strongly, the wine glasses rattled.

'Jesus,' said Nigel, pulling away and rubbing at his arm. 'You've got some kind of freak power.'

Laura grinned, wider this time. 'Crumbly Fudge?' she asked, thrusting the bowl under his nose.

The next morning, Laura's head was a little spacey. She put it down to the wine and got up to use the loo. On the way to the bathroom she trod on something cold and squishy, then promptly banged her thigh against some kind of table that definitely wasn't there when she went to bed. On closer inspection, she realised it wasn't a table but an artist's easel, and she'd trodden on a tube of oil paint.

She did have these things but stashed away at the back of her wardrobe with the vague notion that one day she would actually paint something. Shaking off the sleep, she realised that there was a painting on the easel—a very good painting of her old family cat, Boris. There he was, orange stripes and all, gazing longingly into their pond at Granville Avenue, watching the dancing tadpoles. The light reflection was incredible, and it was so life-like it could've been a photograph. Did she paint it in her sleep? She couldn't remember doing that. She looked down at her hands, turning her palms uppermost. They were streaked in orange oil paint. She remembered that she wished for that. When she was 13, she'd wished to be able to paint. It was true—her wishes were being granted.

She thought about Robin on the track and field, legs flexing, feet pounding in the dirt in time with her own heartbeat. Surely that wish wouldn't be granted, would it? The longing was strong. More powerful than any wish for sweets or arm wrestling or artistic ability. Robin Godiver. She'd tried to keep that name out of her head for so long, but here it was again as vivid as ever before.

Another work day. Laura practised her newfound art skills on Mrs Emmersley's file. She found she could easily capture the image of her secret crush, imagining how Robin would look now, 20 years on from their schooldays. Flawless, as expected. Doodling with impressive ability helped her blot out the never-ending munching of Bulgy Brian and allowed her to daydream of her other life. The life that she should've had, where she would've signed cheques as Mrs Robin Godiver in her practiced hand.

Her phone light flashed. She thought about not answering it. She didn't have to stay in this dead-end job any more. She could get work as an artistic arm-wrestler, join a travelling circus or something. Eyeing the tiny writing inside the card, she answered the call.

'Thank you for calling Port Holland. You're speaking to Laura. How can I help?'

'Laura? This is Aaliyah from reception. You better get down here. This is even weirder than yesterday with that little guy in green.'

'What's going on?' asked Laura, but her line was dead.

Rushing out of the office towards the lifts, all Laura could think about was the wishes. How gloriously ridiculous this whole thing was. Anything or anybody could be waiting for her. Her head filled up again with Robin Godiver and all the ways she had imagined the two of them together. Her whole secondary school experience seemed to be immersed in Robin. Nothing else was important. Robin was her whole world. She couldn't remember anything else she might've wished for. Did the elf-man say five wishes? She'd had the sweets, the arm wrestle and the painting—two left. Maybe Robin would take up two? She should've checked the terms and conditions.

Robin Godiver was indeed in the lobby, but she was not alone. The goddess of the athletic field grinned down at Laura, showing her perfectly straight white teeth. Laura's knees went weak as she watched the love of her life brush an imagined fly from a bare-skinned arm. An arm that Laura had longed to kiss a thousand times over.

'Did anyone wish for a horse?' Robin asked, her voice as honeyed as Laura remembered, and the beautiful white steed she was astride whinnied joyfully.

Falls

Geetha Nair G

He was slumped on a wrought-iron seat under a shady tree. In front of him towered the Indian Institute for Advanced Study. Shimla in May wasn't exactly cool or pretty. Like his wife without make-up, he thought with a surge of bitterness. His wife had insisted on the Shimla trip and on his accompanying her. An old school friend of hers lived in Shimla. Her daughter was in the process of getting wedded. The prolonged festivities had tired him out. He had taken a break. The IIAS was one of his favourite places. History in stone—its grandeur, its well-kept gardens, its air bristling with stories of a bygone era...

He gazed at the windows. Silhouetted behind one of them, he saw a face in profile. He sat up. Sudha? The shape of the chin, the set of the head, the long neck... No. He was imagining things. These days he thought of her often. He did not know why. Thirty years is a long time.

Sudha moved quickly away from the library window. Yes, it was Ravi. He had changed much, but when he looked up, all doubts had been dispelled. A long time, 30 years...

Sudha and Ravi had been classmates. Masters in Economics, Delhi. They had been drawn to each other by their lost state—they had come from far-flung districts to the capital city and shared a love for reading. Soon the love had spilled over from books to each other. She fell under the spell of his eloquence, his Gandhian ideals, his dreams. One dream was to join the civil services, to serve his land. He persuaded her to join the coaching classes along with him. In those days, there were hardly any coaching centres. Civil services coaching had not yet boomed as an industry. They went to a venerable retired officer who conducted classes in his home-cum-coaching centre. Every evening, after university, the two of them would walk to the coaching class. They had chosen English literature as their advanced subject mainly because it was what the old gentleman handled best. And, of course, both of them loved reading English novels.

Learning was one thing, reading for enjoyment, another. She tired of the constant dinning, the grappling with names and movements.

'Why did you drag me into this?' She moaned one evening as they were walking towards the dark steps that led to the road. By way of answer, he laughingly quoted a line from Marlowe's *Dr Faustus*, which had been analysed that day: 'It is a comfort to the wretched to have companions in misery.'

Ravi had been fascinated by the play, by the scholar who had sold his soul to the Devil in return for 24 years of knowledge and power. 'A fine bargain,' he had said to her, smiling, 'especially as we don't believe in devils!'

They stopped on the steps and melted into each other's arms. This was their routine. She never let him get beyond kisses on her face and on her midriff, though he could feel her desire in the way her body arched and her breath quickened. He would stroke and kiss her flat, white midriff in desperation and exclaim, 'Floundering in the bloody English Channel with no hope of reaching England or France!' He blamed it on her deadly convent education. She would only smile in reply.

He cleared the exams. She did not.
He made it to the List. Bihar was to be his promised land. 'Learn Bihari. I'll be back soon to get you,' he smiled as they parted with lingering kisses. He wrote her letter after letter from marvellous Mussoorie. Meanwhile, she had found a job as a lecturer in a college not far from her ancestral home.

Then came his first posting—Bhagalpur. He promised her silk saris in different shades of pink and evenings by the Ganga. 'But aren't we cotton lovers?' she wrote back. As the days went by, though, he wrote less and less about themselves, more and more about the places he visited, the people he met, the challenges he faced.

The letters grew fewer and cooler. Oddly enough, she kept remembering the teenage days spent in the custody of her grandmother. Supper was invariably rice gruel. When she was late, her grandmother rebuked her, saying, 'Once it loses its heat and warmth, it's fit only for the cows.'

She was expecting the blow when it landed. He was getting married to the daughter of an industrialist based near Patna. It was straight out of a commercial movie—this right royal ditch. The letter continued: *What is being in love, after all? Just the fruit of suggestion, circumstance and utility. Just a solution to loneliness and lust. An illusion doomed to be wrecked on the rocks of reality.*

He had always been a good debater. At the very end of the letter were two words that struck her as ludicrous—*Forgive me.*

She put Ravi behind her as resolutely as she had her parents, who had died when she was still a teenager.

Sudha immersed herself totally in her academic pursuits. At 40, she was the most respected and reputed professor in her area of specialisation. She had now moved to the prestigious central university in her neighbouring state. It was on the outskirts of the city.

Learning how to drive a car had become a necessity. She visited a driving school. The owner-instructor was a muscular man in his 30s. His appraising look brought colour to her face. She wanted to walk out, but something rooted her to the spot. The driving lessons began. The instructor was called Hari. Mornings and evenings, he would drive up in his old car and take her through winding by-lanes and gradually through the bustling city roads. His strong hairy forearms emerging from the rolled-up sleeves, the scent of cigarette smoke and something else that he emitted, his eyes on her—everything aroused in her a wild sweetness.

Her mastery of driving paralleled his mastery of her. In two weeks he accomplished what Hitler could not in several years. In another month, she was the possessor of both her driving licence and her marriage certificate.

For several days, she dwelt in a dreamland. There were only Hari's voice and body there. Slowly the dream turned misty and vanished. She awoke. She realised she had made a gross mistake.

Sudha went back to the window. He was still there. She walked downstairs and went up to him. He was dozing. She saw the changes that time had punished him with—the balding head, the bulging stomach. Why was there no taste of ashes in her mouth? Her eyes took in the expensive shirt, the shoes, the huge watch on his thick wrist. In her memories, he wore his trademark khadi kurta and Kolhapuri chappals. She stood undecided awhile. Then she turned and walked away swiftly. The rustle of her cotton sari must have woken him. He saw her unmistakable shape walking away from him, much like Eurydice from Orpheus.

But they were fated to meet that very night. Sudha had parked her car at the usual spot. Next to her was a BMW. From it issued a steady stream of invective delivered in a woman's voice. It was about not knowing how to handle drivers, stupidity, cupidity and so on, delivered in scathing English. Though she was accustomed to verbal abuse, Sudha was shocked. She instinctively glanced at the occupants of the car as she was raising the glass. Ravi and a woman! Of course it had to be his wife, that slim, heavily-made up vixen sharing the back seat. The expression on Ravi's face hurt Sudha. It was that of one who had sold his soul.

A fountain of pity rose up in her for this man whom she once loved so deeply.

Sudha's husband had staggered up to the car by now. He held liquor bottles in both his hands. Sudha got out of the car to open the door for him. It was then that Ravi saw her. He stared at her with shocked, unbelieving eyes. For a long moment, their eyes locked. Then, his dropped. On his lap, she saw a fluffy dog that he was trying in vain to hold down.

It is a comfort to the wretched to have companions in misery, she mused, as she started the car and drove down the hill.

Olya's Kitchen

Helen Harris

People sometimes said that my grandmother, Babushka Olya, did not have blood in her veins but beetroot borscht. What sort of borscht it might be was never mentioned—a winter borscht made with beef stock, bacon fat and garlic or a chilled summer borscht served with dill, hard-boiled egg and sour cream. But to me, as a boy, it made sense. My Babushka Olya smelt of the kitchen. She expressed her love for us, her puzzling English grandchildren, through her cooking, and perhaps that was the best way because other forms of communication sometimes let her down.

Babushka Olya lived in a small flat, five minutes' walk away from our home in Ealing (seven with shopping bags). When my parents bought the house, my mother had apparently put her foot down about Babushka Olya moving in with us. 'There's not room,' she liked to quote herself as saying to my father, 'for me and your mother under the one roof'—which struck me as strange back then because Babushka Olya was very small and my mother, Miranda, only of normal size. Now, of course, as an adult, I understand her. How incredibly infuriating it must have been to have her kitchen and her home taken over by Babushka Olya and her cooking, to have her children fattened up on old-fashioned dumplings and *blini*, Russian buckwheat pancakes. It was the nineties, and my mother would far rather we were eating granola and hummus and alfalfa sprouts.

When Babushka Olya was banished—as she no doubt saw it—from the family home, she did not protest or make a fuss; that was not her way. Instead, she simply ignored the intention behind my mother's veto and set about doing exactly what she had wanted all along. Her small flat was no more than a place she slept and occasionally had tea and saucerfuls of homemade jam with a couple of other older Russian women, who had followed their ambitious children to the West and found themselves stranded in the gastronomic wasteland of London W5. The rest of the time Babushka Olya spent in our kitchen.

Because she was so obviously motivated only by goodness, by her limitless love for my sister Emma and me, it was very hard to stop her. She would arrive without fail about an hour before lunchtime, labouring with her heavy shopping bags, let herself in with our key, which she wore on a cord around her neck, and call out in English and Russian, '*Allyoh? Allyoh? Eta ya.* Is me.'

'Who else?' My mother would sigh—if she happened to be at home—rolling her eyes heavenwards, 'Who else?'

Babushka Olya spent the rest of the day cooking. She made our lunch and dinner, and sometimes uncalled-for extras—great batches of *pel'meni*, delicious little pasta parcels stuffed with beef and pork; *kissel*, a blancmange-like fruit purée which must be the ultimate comfort food; and endless unforgettable *pirogi*, pies.

When it was time to eat, she would summon us. She called me 'Kolya', although my real name is Nicholas or Nick. She called Emma by her name, there being no Russian diminutive for Emma, and I think the fact she had a special name for me made us just that bit closer. We would sit down at a beautifully laid table, and we always had napkins.

My mother fumed and fought back. But she worked full-time as a successful solicitor and was almost always out, so there was not much she could do. My father's job in broadcasting involved much less regular hours. He was often at home between his shifts, but he did not seem to mind his mother's constant presence and was perfectly content with her cooking.

My mother and my grandmother waged war in the fridge. My mother bought all the healthy stuff she preferred us to eat—yoghurt and salads and carrot sticks and dried mango for snacks. But my grandmother would move them to the back of the fridge, behind her pots and jars, where they were forgotten until they spoilt.

When I was 10 and Emma 12, our Babushka Olya suddenly died. Her death was unexpected, yet completely in character. She had shown no signs of illness that any of us had noticed, maybe puffing a little more than usual with her shopping bags. But she had not complained of anything and it was a terrible shock to all of us when, after preparing a big batch of *pel'meni*, she did not put them on to cook but told us that she had a bad pain and needed to lie down. Before the ambulance men arrived, she was dead.

For us children, it was the first death, after which, as Dylan Thomas wrote, 'there is no other.' We were devastated and, I think, also afraid we would go hungry. We had never seen our father cook—Babushka Olya shooed him away if he ever came into the kitchen—and our mother was hardly ever at home. I still remember how, that night, after the undertaker's men had taken Babushka Olya away, we collected in the kitchen, even though none of us really felt like eating, and found Babushka Olya's last batch of *pel'meni* still waiting to be cooked. Even my mother dabbed her eyes as she looked at the rows of little doughy parcels lined up on the worktop, all painstakingly pinched together.

As we stood there, at a loss, my mother did an amazing thing. She said, 'I'll cook them. I owe it to Olya.'

'But you don't know how to,' my father said. 'Do you?'

My mother rolled her eyes, which she liked to do and said, 'P-lease. I've seen her do it often enough.'

She got out the deep saucepan our grandmother used for *pel'meni* and set about cooking them, wearing Babushka Olya's apron to protect her work suit from splashes. The truth is, although *pel'meni* are fiddly to make, cooking them is actually pretty easy—you just drop them into boiling salted water and wait until they rise to the surface. Then you eat them with sour cream, butter and lemon juice, all of which Babushka Olya had left ready for us in the fridge.

We sat at the kitchen table eating them and crying. Of course, they didn't taste quite the same as usual, but then none of us really felt hungry or maybe it was the extra salt from our tears.

Our lives changed after Babushka Olya's death. That summer, I turned 11, and in the autumn I started secondary school. It was a new stage, and the loss of Babushka Olya and her cooking became part of the wider change.

Meals at home changed too—for the worse—although we never actually went hungry. No one knew how to make the dishes Babushka Olya used to make. My mother certainly wouldn't have wanted to, and my father didn't know how. Instead, our diet changed to a pretty typical English menu of sausages, fish fingers and beans when my father was cooking, and things made of tofu and Quorn and weird grains on the rare occasions when our mother took charge. We also ate a lot of convenience food and takeaways, which Babushka Olya had always scorned, and afterwards my poor father would often suffer from indigestion which was, I guess, guilt-induced.

I think, in some ways, after Babushka Olya's death, we stopped being a fully functional family. It was as if she, despite her small size, had been the magnetic force which drew us all together. After her death, it felt as if we were just four people living in the same house, but each leading our own separate life. Meals were eaten quickly, the table unset, and we often ate separately, too, when it suited our own schedules, rather than as a family, all together.

For Emma and me, of course, the major part of our lives then was school. The changes which had taken place at home seemed less significant as we grew up, and our attention was focused more and more on our friends and our lives beyond the family. Occasionally, though, we would eat at a friend's house where traditional, lovingly prepared meals were still served, and we would experience a sharp pang of nostalgia for what we had lost.

To tell the truth, apart from our lost childhood, Emma and I did not have much in common by then. She was two years ahead of me at school, very focused and high-achieving. Our parents were overjoyed when she got a place to study law at Cambridge and looked set to follow in our mother's footsteps. I was not all that academic; I was one of those kids who endured school rather than enjoyed it. My marks were usually pretty mediocre, and our parents would regularly and despairingly wonder aloud what would become of me.

Despite their dire predictions, I made it to university, but I didn't like it there. I could never see the point of all those lectures and essays, which seemed to me to have nothing to do with the real world. A term into my second year, I dropped out and—to my parents' horror—took a job in a restaurant kitchen. Initially, I don't think I was particularly drawn to cooking. I just wanted to show my parents that I could be independent and support myself even without their sacred university education. But in the restaurant—it was a French restaurant called Le Bon Viveur—I discovered something I was actually good at. There, I also met my girlfriend, Irina, a

Russian-speaking waitress newly arrived from Latvia. Irina was beautiful, and she believed in me. She had no hang-ups about the value of a university education. She saw that I was good, better than anyone else at Le Bon Viveur, to be honest, and she pushed me to train as a chef.

The food truck was Irina's idea too. We used to walk home from work every night across the King's Cross redevelopment, and we would see all these fancy food trucks locked up for the night, which served all sorts of cool cuisines during the day. Once, as we walked home in the early hours, Irina took my hand and said, 'Kolya, why don't we get one of those?' Nowadays Irina is the only person who calls me Kolya.

I doubt if the idea of the food truck would ever have got off the ground if it had not been for two things. One was that my parents found it so socially embarrassing that their son worked in a restaurant kitchen that the idea of a fashionable food truck seemed a step up. They even, gratifyingly, knew of the son of friends who worked in a food truck despite a Classics degree from Oxford. The other was that no one can really resist Irina.

So, my parents gave me a loan, and two years ago, after all the inevitable initial hassle and bureaucracy, we started our food truck, serving authentic Russian food. The truck was a bold red and shiny. We named it 'Kolya's Kanteen'.

From the day we opened, we were amazingly successful. There are a lot of Russians in London these days, and from the start we had quite a lot of them coming up to sample our *pirogi* and *pel'meni* and see how they compared to what they remembered from back home. But I don't think it was the Russians who made us such a success story. (We even got a write-up in 'Time Out'.) All the other trucks were serving cool cutting-edge stuff—jazzed up pizzas and curry-infused burgers and fish tacos. There we were, in our retro-looking red truck, serving what Babushka Olya made, and people loved it. Plus, of course, Irina drew the crowds. No one in any of the other food trucks was anywhere near as beautiful as Irina.

Recently, I was thinking how pleased my Babushka Olya would be if only she could see me dishing out *pel'meni* and *blini* and *pirogi* to the people from all over the world queueing up, and I know for sure she would love Irina.

But, thinking about it a bit more, I wasn't sure how thrilled Babushka Olya would actually be. After all, she believed in sitting down to eat at a properly laid table with napkins, and she would never ever have approved of eating in the street. I realised what I have to do next. When we have made enough money from the truck—I repaid my parents' loan already—we are going to open a restaurant, a real, proper restaurant serving traditional Russian dishes. It will have exactly the right décor and ambience. I will have waitresses who are very polite and just a tiny bit strict, and I will call it 'Olya's Kitchen'.

Kashmir Valley's Soofiya Bano

Humra Quraishi

Those shots of the Srinagar home of academic Agha Ashraf Ali—father of the legendary Kashmiri poet Agha Shahid Ali—more than relayed the 'flood fury' of 2014 and its devastating imprints. As more of those pictures lay splashed in the various publications, nostalgia tightened its hold. I not just read aloud lines from Agha Shahid Ali's 'Country Without a Post Office' but also crawled further into the ever tightening folds of nostalgia and recalled all those earlier occasions when I had seen his bungalow from close quarters. I'd sat in the front covered veranda, in the drawing room, in the garden…I had also walked around the fruit trees growing in the compound. And, on more than one occasion, Agha Ashraf Ali had plucked numerous apples from those trees … slicing rather too effortlessly before serving them.

And as we had neared the gates of his home, situated in the Raj Bagh locality of Srinagar, not too far from where the Jhelum flows, he'd gazed at those gates and spoken of his late wife, 'I loved her. We were happy here. She and me. She was from Uttar Pradesh and me from here! What an Avadhi and Kashmiri combination! You know, at times I feel she's not dead and gone…as though she's still around…her soul right here! See these front gates, it still carries her name…Read her name, can you?'

Nostalgia intensifying, as around the same time not too far from those gates, I had met a middle-aged woman who had looked more than determined of the road she was taking, seemingly taking her to a nowhere of sorts. Yet she seemed more than confident to continue walking along the set terrain.

I'd met her rather too accidentally, close to a rundown chai café in Raj Bagh. A sudden downpour, and before I could decide whether to halt under a sprawling Chinar tree or run towards the café, she stood right there, looked towards me and burst out. Offloading. She waits under that Chinar for her teenaged son. Repeatedly saying she waits at the set spot, looking neither left nor right, only straight ahead, her gaze unmoving, just in case she could spot him.

No, she didn't seem to realise the futility of the exercise, even as she'd detailed, 'My son was last seen here, next to this chai café! It's from this spot he was picked up by the devils of the day…yes, the security creatures…they dragged him to the *hukumat*'s interrogation centre.' She had continued mumbling, even as I'd thrown those heartless queries at her: Was her son a militant or a terrorist? Was he an informer or a threat? Camouflaging or carrying crucial information?

'No, no…he very simple. Going to college and back. Not saying this because he's Begum Soofiya Bano's son!'

'Your name Soofiya?'

'I'm Begum Soofiya Bano.'

'But his wife also...'

'Whose?'

'Was visiting someone here in Raj Bagh, his dead wife's name also Soofiya...strange nah! Was wondering that maybe ...'

'Many people with the same name but different destinies!'

'But ...'

'Please...please! Have *reham* on me! I'm nobody's wife!'

'But your son...er, your child...how?'

'Raised him all by myself, whatever best I can do with my very limited resources...doing embroidery on shawls till my eyes couldn't cope with the strain of coming up with complicated designs!'

'But your son...'

'Allah can't take him away like this. This child was gifted to me years back by Allah!'

'How...gifted?'

'Found my baby years back, wrapped up in a shawl, on the shikara taking me along the backwaters to the Dal Lake! Not left him for a single day ever since that day. My child, he is...only mine! No marriage, nothing for me...just me and my child...till those beastly *sarkari* devils dragged him away!'

I'd met hundreds of mothers in the Kashmir Valley, wailing and waiting for their missing sons, but with Begum Soofiya Bano I'd developed a certain rapport. And now, with the news reports of the flood fury hitting the Valley, I tried to get in touch with her.

Though almost certain that with the flood waters wrecking homes and outer roads and inner lanes of the Raj Bagh locality, she couldn't have been around. Definitely not on that particular road of Raj Bagh—one of the worst-affected locales of the Srinagar city—where she had spent months awaiting the return of her missing son.

I couldn't curb the temptation to call her. Her mobile did ring, but there seemed no one at the other end. After a couple of days, even that hazy hope of connectivity diminished. What with the flood waters affecting all possible modes of connection. The cables and lines, snapped. That remote chance of trying to establish contact with her seemed over and done with. Giving up, certain that she and her efforts must have died down by now, I was more than surprised to receive a call from her.

'My son with me! My son with me!' Her shrill voice exclaimed.

'What! Floods washing away hundreds and here you are!'

'He's with me...he came swimming in these flood waters.'

'What! What's all this you saying?'

'Yes, yes...He came swimming...swimming out of that hell hole...that jail where the *hukumat* had thrown him... those bloody beasts had almost tried to kill him, but Allah kept him alive! Allah has once again given him to me!'

'What?'

'We running away from here!'

'Where would you go?'

'Running away from this *jahannum*...my son and I running away in this *sailaab*...these waters coming to our rescue...we out of here!'

'Where?'

'Running from here...anywhere where my son and I could be left alive and not killed.'

'Where to?'

'Maybe towards Avadh or maybe still further...'

'What! All the way there?'

'Maybe...yes...'

'But you're from Kashmir, going all the way there! How?'

'Flowing along with destiny...along with destined turns and also...'

The line got disconnected.

Connection snapped.

Indigo Blue

Jayshree Misra Tripathi

It was an odd request. The email arrived on a Friday afternoon, with the first monsoon downpour. The city certainly needed the respite after the sultry, humid summer. The hostess was well-known for her idiosyncrasies yet was charming enough to entice a faithful group of followers—or were they hangers-on!

> You are cordially invited to a Storytelling session, from 4–8 pm, at my residence. Creative non-fiction, 15 minutes to read aloud. Wear an outfit from your story, and please stay for dinner! Please Note: You must email the final draft to me 24 hours prior to the event.

I was not planning to go anywhere over the weekend, so replied that I would be delighted to attend. What would I write?

Sifting through documents on my desktop and skimming through unfinished drafts, I drifted across to the kitchen for a cup of aromatic Blue Tokai Vienna Roast coffee. *Mmm.* Coffee brewed just right was balm for a busy, multi-tasking mind.

Befuddled, rather, on occasion! Life had dealt its blows, but I kept getting up.

After pulling open my one and only set of Chesterfield drawers for some handwritten notes on stories yet to be woven, I came across some yellowed pages at the bottom of one.

Handwritten.

This is the tale of the Bhanja Princess, Vakula Mahadevi, second in line to the throne, of the Widow Warrior Queens of Kalinga.

I re-read my notes:

The Bhaumakaras of Utkala came to power around 736 CE and ruled until 950 CE, protecting Buddhism, Shaivism and Vaishnavism, a period often referred to as the golden age of Orissa. Religious traditions came to be reconciled, creating a deep interest in Tantrism and Tantric Buddhism. Philosophy, art, literature, architecture and administration flourished under their rule. Scholars and priests visited lands across the seas. The dynasty had six reigning queens who, according to tradition, were widows at ascension. Talk about empowered women—from centuries ago!

I began to type.

The next afternoon, I began my story. Last in the queue. There were seven of us. I licked my lips, slightly nervous in front of 20 distinguished guests, many of whom were writers, some from overseas.

We had been served a welcome drink of crushed berries and herbs, in a copper tumbler, with a piquant taste. Sweet and sour, garnished with mint leaves and slices of lemon, slivers of almonds—and a touch of aniseed perhaps? Why did Agatha Christie's 'Arsenic and Old Lace' flit across my mind? Arsenic was odourless, so I heaved a sigh of relief.

Our hostess called it her 'mystery drink'!

I wore an indigo-blue crisp cotton saree with a white blouse, *kajal* in my eyes and my hair pulled back into a rustic knot. Brown lipstick and copper hoop earrings seemed just right for my story. I had even gone to a salon for temporary henna tattoos, divinely created all over my hands! Even the fangs of a snake that crept insidiously from my saree blouse, half-sleeved, and ended near my ring finger, added to the nature of my tale!

The incense sticks had been lit for over three hours now, and the heady mixture of jasmine and sandalwood clouds, swirling near the large main oil lamp and the dozen diyas at the head of the body, assailed the senses. Vakula Mahadevi glanced at the still corpse of her stepdaughter, draped in a simple yellow cotton saree denoting her 'virgin' status, appalled at the deathly hue of her face and hands. No amount of sandalwood paste and henna applied on her palms and hands, in intricate designs and tiny lotus blossoms, could quite disguise this. The maids had first placed the body on the floor, with the head pointing towards the north, the direction for the 'dead'. Then they had discreetly bathed the body, wiped it dry gently and placed it on a mat. Following the traditional rituals, the next was the application of sandalwood paste. The yellow saree was draped on the body and red *alataka* liquid applied around the soles of her feet, symbolic of her status as a young, unmarried queen.

The handmaidens whispered incessantly, their faces swollen with tears, as they performed the delicate task of adornment of the dead body while disguising the deadly signs of poison. The handmaidens gently pulled the dead queen's hands straight beside her body, as required, and slipped on a dozen gold bangles through each wrist. Pearl and gold necklaces, with large red rubies and emeralds, were placed around the neck of the dead queen. Jasmine and marigolds were strewn along the silhouette of the corpse— so still, so serene, it seemed she was just asleep.

'Hurry up,' Vakula Mahadevi admonished the maids, 'the pandits will be here soon.' The virgin queen, Dandi Mahadevi, should be ready before the priests arrived to perform the last rites. The administrative durbar would accompany them, and Vakula Mahadevi would have to step behind the muslin purdah, as custom dictated, together with the other princesses of the royal palace. Her lips curled in disdain. It was over. The Bhaumakara dynasty would end with this death, and she, a Bhanja princess from the neighbouring *rajya*, would ascend the throne. But this was not the time to show any sign of cheer.

Vakula Mahadevi stepped forward and placed a few grains of uncooked rice on the dead queen's mouth, followed by a few drops of the holy *ganga jal*, from the *kansalota*, for the soul to attain liberation. It was also believed to appease the soul, which would now begin the journey of transmigration. She also placed some holy tulsi leaves on the right-hand side of the corpse, and as she drew back, she could have sworn there was a slight quiver in the bluish hand. The sages had pronounced her death, but was she truly dead? And who would have dared to poison her? The two elderly handmaidens were loyal and had served the dead queen since her birth. They remained with her when she was declared queen, after her mother Gauri Mahadevi's death. Vakula Mahadevi had not even been considered for the position—at that time. Now, she would be anointed queen. Yet the constant fear remained—of being poisoned. Whom could she trust amongst the handmaidens? The few close to her heart were no more. Apprehensive of an imminent plot, she refused a glass of *chaas*, sour buttermilk, brought in her personal gold goblet.

The previous queen, Gauri Mahadevi, had taken no chances upon her failing health and had a decree drawn up and attested, even declared in all corners of the kingdom, proclaiming her daughter, Dandi Mahadevi, Vakula Mahadevi's stepdaughter, as her successor. No one had opposed her decree. The neighbouring *rajya*s had sent messengers welcoming the queen designate. Vakula Mahadevi's family had also sent congratulatory messages and gifts. It had surprised her then, but now she began to understand their vision.

Vakula Mahadevi did not hate her late husband's daughter. As she was brought into the palace on her palanquin after her marriage, a very young bride, she was welcomed warmly by her stepdaughter. She instinctively realised that she must remain friendly with both the mother and daughter to maintain cordial relations with her husband, King Subhakara V.

This ascension of a widowed woman as the queen, one who would rule in her own right and not as a regent for a minor heir, was unique in the land of Bharat. Vakula Devi wanted to be a part of the cultural heritage of the Bhaumakaras. Her childhood companion's brother was now one of the three elders, the revered Brahmin priests, whose advice was sought for every political decision. The Buddhist elders were also revered, but as their teachings were not inclined towards warfare, their blessings were sought only for religious festivities.

The only disturbing news were the whispers in the corridors of the palace—that she had planned to usurp her stepdaughter. Three mendicants had been summoned by the Brahmin elders and the diwans. They had been escorted to different chambers and were unaware of the others' presence. Each had been brought at different times to examine the virgin queen in the presence of the elders and two elderly handmaidens, one of whom was loyal to Vakula Mahadevi. Covertly so, it was whispered, in the corridors of the palace and the women's quarters, but even her most efficient of spies were unable to gather enough proof of this.

The elders had decided that the virgin queen's demise was to be described as untimely, due to a debilitating consumption. There would be no talk of poison, and the handmaidens were instructed to deftly weave intricate patterns with henna and sandalwood paste over every portion of her body to hide any indications and tattoo any discolourations.

The mourners would not be allowed to come too close to her body, but garlands of marigolds would be hung from columns that would be deemed as markers from where to pay last respects.

Vakula Mahadevi smiled, then gasped in pain. Blood oozed from her ankle. She glanced down at her foot, at the deadly snake that slithered away, then, in anguish, at the handmaidens who made no effort to hold her as she slithered to the ground. The elderly handmaidens stood very still. The deed was done. They had remained loyal to their virgin queen.

Nodding at each other, they smeared kohl into their eyes so that tears flowed profusely.

Their wails brought the guards stumbling into the chamber, where they immediately formed a circle around Vakula Mahadevi, lying in pain on the floor. The two handmaidens were escorted out of the chamber and through the corridors to the far east of the palace, then down stone steps into the punishment chamber. Their protests were in vain. Cuffed by their legs to heavy iron chains that hung from the dark, foul-smelling dungeon, they sighed, unsure of their fate.

Justice had been served. Their loyalty, unflinching, in the face of certain death. Only one last chess piece had to fall into place—naming Vakula Mahadevi as the one who had dared to poison a rival royal.

The eldest of the palace Brahmins entered the dungeon with a retinue of guards. The handmaidens shivered in fear. He was a favourite of Vakula Mahadevi; the favours and lands that had been bestowed on him were whispered about in the corridors of the minions with raised eyebrows.

'You will not be pardoned for the snake that bit our Widow Warrior Queen to-be nor will you be sent into exile. I will pray that your souls are forgiven for the treacherous accusations about our Vakula Mahadevi.'

The handmaidens, with their lowered heads, begged for mercy.

Two younger handmaidens entered with a mud pot filled with sandalwood paste. They gently pressed the women to lie down and prised their hands apart.

Then, as they began to smear the paste lovingly into their elder soul-sisters arms and legs, their faces and necks, they began to moan softly, crying gently in a haunting litany.

The head guard motioned a waiter to take forward the copper lotas, with their small spouts, and watched as water was poured into each quivering mouth.

Dusk fell as these processes were coming to an end. The priest turned away, muttering slokas under his breath, counting his tulsi beads. The guards followed, and they left as silently as they had entered.

The four handmaidens looked deeply into each other's eyes.

After that, it was just a matter of time. The guilty handmaidens were last seen asleep, their bodies stained a strange indigo blue.

I sighed. There was a long pause.

I smiled and looked up. The room was macabre dark! Just what I wanted!

Then, I was suddenly struck by severe abdominal pain, but I couldn't cry out! I was very thirsty and hoarse, yet unable to ask for water, as I just could not utter any words. Nor could I wipe the beads of sweat on my brow, as I felt faint.

The audience clapped, hesitantly, wondering if I had finished my tale.

I hadn't, as I had planned to draw the audience into the conclusion with their feedback so that 'The End' would be a joint venture! A creative ending to an unusual tale of non-fiction.

Why had my hands turned indigo blue? Was that blood oozing from the snake tattoo fangs? Was that a vision of Vakula Mahadevi frowning at me? Was it my hostess trying to smother me? No, no, that's unfair. Besides, what would she gain from my loss?

That is the last thing I recalled before I passed out.

But I heard voices. Was it my imagination? Were the stories I wrote of parallel lives? Had my words been uttered in a past life? The voices just assured me not to be afraid and the answers would come in time.

I came to and received another round of applause, but there was a knot in my stomach. It had taken over an hour to wake up from my dreams. Memories of past lives?

My hostess apologised profusely, wringing her bejewelled hands back and forth—it was meant to be the grand finale, no harm intended! Just a few herbs to make me sleepy and basically faint, with no risk to my health.

Indeed.

The incident shook me more than I cared to admit.

I stayed low for a couple of weeks until friends started dropping by. I had to answer the door. They just wouldn't leave. Finally, I agreed to go for counselling. I cancelled that quietly. Decided to go for a regressive therapy session instead.

The ancient Greek philosopher Plato averred that knowledge gained in past lives is the basis of education in the present. Wise Plato!

Transmigration of souls? I was getting curiouser and curiouser....

Stories unravelled in whispers. Is the imagination unbound in its possibilities of rebirth, past lives woven in a kaleidoscope of memories, snatches of conversation, once spoken or perhaps overheard? I floated way back in time, in sorrow, in great joy…yet I was always in pain. The poison? The snakebite? Did I die many unnatural deaths? The gentle tap on my forehead brought me back to the present. I felt so weary. Unafraid but weary.

I cancelled after 13 sessions. 13. My lucky number. Unlucky for some. I did not want to know more. Two indigo-blue henna spots remained near the fangs of the snake tattoo, even after months. Shades of Lady Macbeth? I stopped worrying.

This time my tale will be set in the present.

In my time.

The Very Narrow House

Latha Anantharaman

Ambi Next Door told this story to Narasimhan, and I heard it from my cousin, who was married to Narasimhan's sister. I don't even know how much of it is true. My cousin tends to embellish, but don't we all? Who knows what goes on in the row houses of Ramapuram? My uncles used to joke that foxes ran in the streets even in the daytime. If you looked into any of those short doorways, all you could see was one shaft of sunlight halfway down the dark corridor, from the open skylight, and the distant white rectangle that was the back doorway. Each house shared a wall with the next, and they all had the same spaces, but as for what happened in those spaces...

It happened in that very narrow house there, the one with a single long window. They were a particularly reclusive family from a village back east, only two generations old in Palakkad. Hardly anyone remembers Hariharan now—he died so long ago. He was some kind of sub-priest at the temple, chiefly engaged to refill the oil lamps. The Ramapuram women didn't know Hariharan's wife, a bride brought from that same village back east. Chellammal was much younger than Hariharan, but a big woman, with a voice as gruff as a man's and eyebrows shaggy and dark. Her sari was hiked halfway up to her knees as she went about her chores. Her thin hair was twisted into a hasty wet tangle and remained that way till far into the afternoon. The other women in the village smeared their legs and arms with turmeric during their baths to keep their skin smooth, but Chellammal had no time for such niceties, and the hair grew thick on her legs. They bathed in the river, but she bathed with well water to save time in the mornings. In Ramapuram, women prided themselves on their well-oiled tresses and radiant skin, and the men were notorious for looking them up and down as they went about their chores. Chellammal was so plain that the men never looked at her a second time.

Hariharan was heard more often than seen, shouting at his wife and son, beating them both until the boy, Murali, grew old enough to jump the back wall and run to the river whenever he felt anger rising in the house. The boy resembled his mother, and maybe that's why Hariharan never took to him.

No one in Ramapuram would consider marrying their daughters into the family, mainly because of the harsh old man but also because they were from back east, where people were known to burn their daughters-in-law. (That's what these villagers used to say about easterners, you understand, I'm sure you're all very nice people.) Another reason was that Murali had a sixth toe on his left foot. He turned his foot awkwardly to hide it and seldom tucked up his *veshti* as the other boys did. It was too inauspicious to talk about, and by the time he was grown, only the old women in the village remembered it. On the rare occasion a girl was suggested for Murali, one of them would lower her voice and say, 'Better not', and the subject was dropped. It was Chellammal's aunt in Tiruchi who collared a girl to serve in the household as wife and servant.

Sharada, an orphan unwanted in her uncle's house, joined the family silently, jumping to it whenever her mother-in-law told her to do something. The two women hardly spoke, but Sharada had followed orders all her life and knew housework. They slipped smoothly in and out of each other's tasks. Very soon, Chellammal's instructions shrank to a word or two. When she simply pointed or tossed her head this way or that, Sharada understood exactly what she needed. At first, whenever the old man insulted his wife, he slid an eye toward Sharada, looking for a hint that she might become his ally, but the girl remained loyal to both mother and son.

It seemed unlikely that two diffident young people would find love in such circumstances, but that is what happened. A steady affection took root between Murali and Sharada, the way a peepul seed germinates between two stones. They were wise enough to hide it inside their nights, communicated even then in caresses rather than whispers. During the day, their eyes never met in front of other people. When she brought him something to drink, she put it down next to him and said in a neutral tone, 'Here's a tumbler of buttermilk.' He never pronounced her name. (What do you mean, who told me that? It doesn't matter, I like to put in something of my own when I tell a story.)

The girl who had married Ambi Next Door was a cheerful local with bright eyes. She often visited her parents a few doors down, where they questioned her about her new neighbour. Every now and then, she tried to engage Sharada in a chat over the wall between their respective backyards. But Sharada could not quite understand the dialect hereabouts, and she made short, confused replies. No one visited them, and the other women in the village knew only what they heard through the common walls—Hariharan's shouting, Chellamma's low replies and the silence of the young couple.

Hariharan came home one afternoon angrier than usual. He had gone to collect a promised measure of rice and returned empty-handed and irrational. He took up the first thing he saw, the wooden *palakai* they placed on the floor, to sit on. He hit Chellammal on the shoulder once and lifted his arm to strike again. But Murali had come up behind him with the other *palakai* and felled Hariharan with one blow on the back of the skull. The neighbours heard it all—the shouting, the screams of the women as the old man hit his wife, the screams again as he fell. Then there was silence.

Murali and Sharada helped Chellammal sit up and checked her shoulder. She waved her hands at them to stop fussing. Her shoulder hurt and it would get worse, but she stood and twitched her sari into place. None of them spoke. The only sound in the kitchen for long minutes was their jagged breathing. Finally, they brought themselves to look at Hariharan. He lay still, and now there were voices from the other side of the wall.

'Mami, has something happened? Murali, shall we come there?'

In a few minutes people would gather. They would first peer into the dim porch and then venture up the corridor and into the *koodam*.

The three standing figures in the room were as silent as the one who lay on the floor. Murali bent and turned the old man face-up without touching his bloody head. By then the neighbours were tiptoeing in over the threshold—Ambi with his father and brothers, Srihari from across the street and others. They squinted against the sunbeam from the skylight and struggled to make out the shape on the floor. It was some time before Ambi Next Door bent his ear to the old man's chest and then held his hand above the slack lips to feel for a breath. He stood up and shook his head.

That was the end of the silence. They all asked questions. Chellammal barely spoke a sentence before she was interrupted with another question. But she had readied her story—'He hit me, and then he slipped and fell. It sounded like he cracked his head against the other *palakai*.'

Srihari asked, 'Where's Murali?'

'Gone to draw water,' Chellammal said.

Somewhere a brass pot clinked against stone. The men noticed Sharada only when she emerged from the darkness of the kitchen, put down a pot of water, murmured something about bringing more and disappeared towards the well.

When she came back with another pot and a cloth, the two women began to wash the blood from the old man's face. The men stood about, not sure what to do. Was he quite dead? Should they call some authority? Or should they consult the senior priest? Someone finally went to look for Murali and brought him in. The three sat stunned while the men talked around them.

The next day, the flag was to be hoisted for the chariot festival, and until the body was cleared, no preparations could be made. The temple could not be opened, and the Lord would remain unfed. There were no elders to speak of in Hariharan's family. Ambi's father, who had hired Hariharan in the first place, took charge, and Murali followed his instructions over the days of rituals that followed.

But the family became more isolated than before. People began to look away instead of greeting Murali. When he or Chellammal looked into the street, it seemed to them that their neighbours turned into their own doorways more abruptly than they used to.

One afternoon, Chellammal went into the kitchen and put her hand inside the third tamarind jar. She pulled out a small cloth bag, thrust it in Murali's hand and whispered urgently to him. She twisted two gold bangles from her wrist and gave him those as well. Sometime after dusk, he stole away from the village. It took two days for Ambi Next Door to notice he was gone. Chellammal told him Murali had gone to see about an old debt, but she wouldn't look him in the eye.

Ambi never saw Murali again, and he never saw any letters come for Chellammal. Ambi's father wrested a minuscule widow's pension from the temple committee for Chellammal, and with that money the two women lived their straitened lives. The widow, wearing an undyed sari, her head shaved and covered, was no more incarcerated than she had been during Hariharan's lifetime. Sharada, miserable for want of Murali, was as silent as ever. Occasionally someone asked after the young man, and then they stopped asking. Hardly anyone saw the women's faces, even Ambi Next Door, who collected their pension for them and paid for their provisions. But for years they felt their every move was noted.

About five years after Hariharan died, Chellammal fell ill. A week-long fever left her limping and struggling to breathe, and her body seemed wasted. She told Ambi Next Door she would go to her aunt's house in Tiruchi, either to recuperate or to die. It was not proper to die here in the village and leave her young daughter-in-law alone. He agreed to bank the pension and watch the house till he heard from them. He put the two women on a train, and that was the last he saw of them for nearly six months.

He was startled in the dark hours of one morning to hear a horse cart from the station draw up near the house. By the time he pulled together his *veshti* and unbolted his front door, Chellammal was sweeping her front step. 'I'll talk to you after we've settled in,' she told him. She seemed recovered and strong. Later in the morning, he brought cooked food for the day's meal and asked what provisions they needed.

The six months away seemed to do Sharada some good as well. There was energy in her step, and she almost smiled sometimes. So my cousin says. By his account, these women were seen only in glimpses as they washed the front threshold or drew water from the well out back. So, did the neighbours actually see a change in her? Or did they simply figure that a visit to a big town with weavers and potters and temples and markets was bound to brighten a woman's eyes?

Chellammal lived much longer than anyone expected after the illness that took her to Tiruchi. The two lived as silently as before. Ambi's wife and mother sometimes saw Sharada drawing water and came near the garden wall to chat. It must have been lonely for a woman living as she did, they thought, with no one but a mother-in-law to talk to. Murali had not been heard of in all that time. But Sharada, on those rare occasions on which she was seen, greeted them with a quick nod and slipped away into the house again.

One morning, more than 20 years after that trip to Tiruchi, Ambi's wife and mother heard Sharada calling out to them, possibly for the first time. Over the wall between the back gardens, she told them that Chellammal had stopped breathing in the night. She had washed and dressed the body by herself and laid it out, not wanting to disturb other women. When they came into the *koodam*, the oil lamp was lit and there was little more to be done. There were no relatives to be informed, nothing to wait for. The temple could not be opened till the body had left the village, so Ambi, Srihari and two other men carried it to the cremation ground within the hour. Sharada was desolate.

After the cremation, Ambi Next Door bathed in the river and came home to sit on the *thinnai* with a tumbler of coffee. Srihari crossed the street to return the paper he had borrowed.

'Strange, wasn't it?' he began.

'What was strange?' Ambi asked.

'She had a sixth toe on her left foot. I never noticed that when she was alive.'

Half an hour later, when Ambi's wife came to call him to lunch, she found him frowning at the floor. His coffee was still in the tumbler, stone cold.

The Closed Cinema

Meena Menon

On the busy Lal Chowk road in Srinagar, the gate was barely visible. It was old and rusted. 'Where is Firdaus Cinema?' I asked a passerby. 'Right here,' he said, pointing to a decrepit gate. I stepped inside, carefully opening a small door in the main gate. It creaked and bits of rusted iron fell down. Ahead was a tall, concrete building, quite ugly. It looked unused and old. The ticket window was closed, but the rates were still scrawled on a blackboard. A wooden chair was propped up against the wall and an old bicycle stood forlornly in front of it. An unwashed man came out from nowhere and said he was the caretaker. 'The theatre is closed for many years,' he announced to no one. I looked around and tried to enter its big hall, but a collapsible iron gate stopped me.

I looked up at the triangular top of the theatre. A pariah kite circled around, whistling. The small ground in front was bare. I stood in disbelief. Not a single theatre in Srinagar was open. The *militants* had closed it. Years ago, people must have come here to watch a movie. There were plush red seats inside, which went back and forth, and popcorn. The gates would be wide open to let the odd car pass through. Huge hoardings would be displayed across the front entrance, advertising the movie. There was a strange sense of desolation now. Even the lone caretaker felt it. This time, he looked at me, saying, 'No one comes here any more. What's the use of an old closed theatre?'

'And what about the owners?' I persisted. The caretaker gave me a long look and sighed deeply. He shook his head, it was almost a shudder.

It was at night that they came for him, almost knocking down the solid wood door of his house. They wore masks, black ones, across their faces. He couldn't remember how many had come. They had big guns. He tried to plead with them. It was useless. He hoped that his wife who was upstairs would not wake up. There was no way of even telling her. The masked men dragged him out. Such brutes. Steel-like arms gripped him around his neck and something like a gun barrel was thrust into his side. It hurt so much. They blindfolded him and shoved him into a vehicle. He sat wedged between the men, and they drove for a long time. No one spoke. He had no idea where he was being taken. He was choking—they had stuffed some cloth into his mouth.

He was terrified. This is how men died here. They were taken away in the night and no one heard of them again. People waited for years, they called them something—ah, yes, the missing persons. Was he going to join their ranks?

And for what? He wanted to laugh. For running a movie theatre? But that was long ago. There was a gurgling sound in his throat—he could not keep down the laughter any more. The brutes shoved him into silence. Finally they got somewhere. It didn't seem very far off but then he lived away from the old city. It was cold—he was shivering under his *firan* (woollen cloak). His hands and sides were bruised and hurt.

They pushed him around for a while. He managed to spit out his gag. 'Where are you taking me?' he spluttered. This time he got a knock on the head. He felt dizzy. His last thought was that he was going to die. When he came to, he was lying between rows of chairs. Everything was dark and silent. His blindfold was removed, but his hands were tied. His gag was back too. His head throbbed with pain. Where am I, what is this place? He could see nothing in the dark, his eyes clouding with blood. He passed out again from the pain and exhaustion. He couldn't remember how long he was there. He remembered waking up hungry and still squashed between the rows of chairs. The first thought that came to him was—Could this be a theatre? A weight lifted from his chest. At least I am in a movie theatre—he smiled despite the pain. He tried to lift himself up, but the space between the chairs was not enough. His hands were stiff with blood. It was still and silent in the dark. There was an awful damp smell. What do they want with me? He lay back on the ground trying to make himself comfortable. After all, it was a movie theatre.

The first time he saw a film was when he was six years old. It was a Tarzan movie. His grandfather had taken him for it. It was rare in those days for people not to see films. This was the era of the movie theatre, not the VCR or DVDs. After school, his grandfather used to wait for him at the theatre—it was near his school. Sometimes his grandfather would not be able to find him in the crowd. They would go to a small hotel and have chai and biscuits, even hot samosas. The memory of the smell of those golden triangles brought saliva to his mouth. He twisted around again, only to feel the intense pain in his hands. And the gag, yes, he was wondering what was stuffed into his mouth—some dirty rag that he chewed on absent-mindedly. What was that film he saw, the one with the chariot race? And who was that actor? His memory was failing him. His thoughts went back to the high excitement during the chariot race. People were standing in their seats and cheering the tall, handsome actor with blue eyes. Oh, what a film it was! Something to do with Jews. He tried playing a game, trying to remember the name from the various scenes that were slowly passing through his dazed mind.

The door opened, letting in a streak of light. His captors were back. He could hear them talking. They were dragging him out of the place feet first. He could not even speak. They blindfolded him, so he guessed that they were taking him somewhere. His entire body hurt, but his groans were muffled by the gag. He kept twisting and turning till he felt the hard poke of a cold steel barrel in his side. No one said anything, they sat in silence. It was freezing—his *firan* was not enough to keep him warm.

The road was winding upwards. No more theatres, he thought to himself, this must be some forest. His thoughts went back to the film—Who was the blond charioteer? He could imagine the rows of trees covered with snow along the road, army men standing like ghosts, wearing their fleece jackets and looking menacing with their guns. He remembered the joke about Johnny Weissmuller, the one who learnt to ride a rhinoceros before he could spell it. Ha ha! One of his movie-mad uncles had told him that. He loved the way Tarzan swung on those vines and later learnt it was possible to do that. He yearned to visit a tropical forest, but all he got was this! He remembered The Firdaus—such a beautiful theatre with its huge concrete pillars. He had named his son after the theatre. Where is Firdaus now? Ah, yes, he was in the US—he used to send him films. The theatre had closed down years ago. Was the place he had gone to The Firdaus? He would never know.

He remembered the day they came to close it down. He couldn't make out who they were. Young men with guns and flowing cloaks. Their sharp eyes missed nothing. It was the last show of some film starring Amitabh Bachchan. It was revived by popular demand. How he loved that movie! He had seen it every time it was shown in the hall. No way— they said to his pleading. Tickets had already been sold and the hall was full. He could sense the excitement, the tense, breathless anticipation as the hall darkened. He was smiling as he fed the film into the projector. That must have all rusted now, he thought, diverted by the loss. They opened the door with their guns pointing at him. 'Shut it down.' He still remembered the grim silence that followed these words. He looked perplexed? He started stuttering in fear. Why on earth? He fell on his knees. Why? Why? He loved The Firdaus more than his wife. It would be a brutal separation. They had hit him then, too, on the side of his head—he was younger then, he could take it. He scrambled on the floor, reaching for their cloaks and trying to grab the edges. He got a kick in his face. He pleaded for mercy. He could hear the crowd getting restless and impatient. Soon they would start shouting. He dreaded what was going to happen. 'Tell them the show is cancelled,' one of the young men ordered.

Such beautiful young men, but no kindness. He looked at them in disbelief, but they were dead serious. Again, the gun was pointed at his head. Slowly, he picked himself up. He made his way down the stairs from the outside. The usher, an old man called Ustad, looked at him in shock. There was blood on his face and on his shawl. He could not even speak. In a low whisper, he gave Ustad the news. The door opened to a raucous scene, people were standing up demanding refunds. Ustad walked to the front. 'The show is cancelled,' he said in hushed tones. More noise, more demands for refund. He felt bad afterwards, leaving Ustad to take the flak. He managed to slink away. The streets were freezing. He wanted the warmth of his house and a *kangri* (a small pot of warm coals carried in a basket). He could not run, he felt so weak. The blood on the side of his face had dried. It was a long walk to his house from old Srinagar.

Suddenly, he found himself being pushed out. It was freezing, and he fell face first on the snow. They were untying his legs. Ah, good, he could walk now. No, they were asking him to kneel. His stiff, old legs struggled on the slippery snow. He tried to swing his hands in a desperate bid for mercy and kept falling over. He suddenly realised what they were going to do. He would never see The Firdaus again or watch a movie. And suddenly he remembered it was Charlton Heston, yes, the charioteer in *Ben Hur* was Heston alright. Shots rang out. As he bent over one last time, there was a half-smile on his face.

Ghost

Meher Pestonji

Kaizad loved acting the ghost. He would flash a torch under his chin, bloody shadows distorting face, howl like a hyena and rush at his four-year-old sister, Natasha. In another avatar, his growling ghost, draped in white sheets, powerful torches beaming out as eyes, would utter her name in blood-curdling snarls, threatening to behead her if she didn't hand over her chocolate. He delighted in plunging the kitchen into darkness, shouting 'power failure', as Tara-tai, the elderly maid, fried fish over a hissing Primus stove. When she threatened him with hot oil, he'd hide behind the water filter to scare Natasha with a loud 'whaaaah'.

His pranks made Mother come rushing, fold the baby in her arms and admonish the chortling boy. Her appeals to Father to rein in the irrepressible 10-year-old met with, 'Boys will be boys. Kaizad will outgrow this.'

The two-storeyed Chinoy house was in a street of dilapidated buildings struggling to hold dignity against the onslaught of inflation. Rust gnawed at wrought-iron balconies. Peepul leaves took root in cracks. Plaster flaked in patches. Yet homemade *torun*s of fresh flowers hung over the entrance each morning as steps to the patio were adorned with welcoming designs of chowk.

At garden level was the kitchen, living room and a tiny office room, with a roll-top teakwood desk, a chair with fading upholstery and a cupboard holding dusty files. The floor above held three bedrooms opening into a narrow corridor at the end of which stood a pendulum clock, with Roman numerals marking time.

A narrow flight of stairs led to the terrace with water tanks and a cobweb-covered attic stacked with paint boxes, trunks and furniture that had fallen into disuse. A room rarely visited except when some unwanted item needed to be junked. It was here that Kaizad brought his ghost story books—to read in an ambiance that matched their tenor. But he didn't read much.

He loved rummaging among discarded treasures, sending a lizard scuttling out of corners. Gingerly sitting on a three-legged chair balanced against a black trunk with 'Hormusji Shiavax Chinai' painted on its side, he'd peer at outdated almanac calendars, auspicious days circled in faded red ink, a broken bottle-opener inlaid with blue stones, ledger-folio-sized diaries filled in a script he did not know, pens with rusted detachable nibs, and dry bottles of Mercurochrome and iodine.

His recent find, his late grandfather's wire-rimmed glasses and dentures, was most exciting. They were in a dust-covered tin of Cadbury's Tiffins on a shelf above the trunks. The box had a paper label, 'Hormusji Shiavax Chinai', in the same stencil as the trunk. He had noticed it almost a year ago, wondering why a box of chocolates had been reserved for his grandfather. But he was neither tall enough to reach it nor strong enough to place one heavy trunk on top of another to climb up.

One day, when Tara-tai remarked, 'Baba is now touching my shoulder,' Kaizad thought he might be able to reach the intriguing box, the only carefully placed object in a higgledy-piggledy room. The shelf was still inches away from his outstretched hand. Climbing the trunk brought the box within reach. As fingers closed around its dusty edge, he lost his balance, crashing to the ground. The box split open, its contents scattering.

The first sight of grinning teeth embedded in pink sent a shiver of disgust down his spine. The dentures sat inches away from his foot, mocking his audacity to disturb. Stifling an impulse to kick them away, he picked them off the ground with the edge of forefinger and thumb, placing them on the three-legged chair, from where they continued to grin.

It felt strange, observing a part of his dead grandfather's body grinning at him. False body, he told himself, struggling with squeamishness.

The hard-brown spectacle case had not opened. It spanned barely five inches in a metal he did not recognise. At the touch of his thumb, its spring snapped opened. And his own eyes stared back at him from two gold-edged rounds. Pulling apart the arms, he adjusted the glasses over his face. Vision blurred, but the dignified glasses made him feel grown up. Lowering the specs and peering over the rim, like Mr Furtado his English teacher, he strutted onto the tiny terrace imitating, 'Friends, Romans, countrymen, lend me your ears....' swishing off the glasses with a flourish as his teacher did in class.

Words trailed off as his eyes again fell on the grinning teeth. They were whiter than Furtado's. While Furtado had an uneven tooth in his lower jaw, these were perfectly aligned. Slowly, Kaizad moved towards the three-legged chair with the teeth. Grandfather's glasses slipped as he bent to examine, then forced himself to take them in hand.

He had anticipated something slimy, but the teeth and the pink they were embedded in were as dry as the tins of paint. Holding the dentures in his palm, he ran a finger over their jagged edge. Did his grandfather smile like this, he wondered, covering the corners of his mouth with his index fingers. How many teeth showed when he spoke? When he got angry? When he laughed? The 10-year-old struggled to visualise the grandfather who had died before he was born.

Next morning, as he stood before the sepia-tinted photograph of his grandfather, with an oil lamp burning before it, performing the daily ritual of 'take Mohtapappa's blessings before going to school', he looked at the image with more curiosity. The dignified man was not too old—50-something—with a broad forehead, bushy eyebrows and a small moustache like his fathers. He was not wearing glasses. The teeth were not visible either.

He wore the traditional Parsi dress—a grey-rimmed *fehto* on his head and a dark *duglo* with gold buttons running down the front. Men of the older generation wore black or brown *dugla*s at formal occasions, unlike today when they wear white *duglee*s with effeminate bow-strings, like ribbons in Natasha's hair. An impish gleam came into his eyes at the thought of his sister. The teeth were perfect to frighten her.

It was Tuesday. Football after school. Kaizad came home at 5:30 instead of 4. As always, a tall glass of milk waited for him on the dining table. Tara-tai had fried hot pakoras for the hungry boy.

'Any homework?' asked mother.

'I finished it in school,' he replied, impatient to be off to the terrace.

'Wash up. Someone's coming to meet you.'

'Meet me?' His tongue, tingling with pakora spices, curling in surprise.

'Your dad's fixed up a tutor.'

'Oh pleeeaase!'

'Mr Sharma is coming to see your books,' she continued, ignoring his protest. 'Tuitions start from Monday.'

Grumpily, Kaizad went to his room and waited for the Sharma he was sure would be odious. When the tutor arrived, he answered in monosyllables. Mother made him bring out his maths books, science book, grammar book, even his Hindi and art books, while the tutor turned pages. 'He is an eighties student. He can be a nineties student. If he works hard, I can get him 98 to 100 per cent in maths,' pronounced the tutor.

At last Kaizad escaped to his room. All day he had been planning to sneak a white sheet to the terrace, fix dentures and glasses on it with scotch-tape, drape it over his head and perfect the ghostly image with a torch under his chin.

It would be grotesque enough to startle Tara-tai and even Mother, he thought gleefully. 'Aiyyyooo!' Tai would scream. Natasha would bawl, running from maid to mum. And Mother, she'd give him a whack and complain to Father, who'd only smile and sympathise. Worth a bellyful of laughs.

Dinner-time conversation was all about the new tutor who'd been recommended by Father's friend. 'Remember, son, your grandfather was a brilliant engineer. As chief engineer of the Western Railways, he was in charge of the entire stretch from Dahanu to Bharuch. During the 29 years of his service, there wasn't a single accident.'

Grandfather was rarely mentioned. Eerie to talk of him the day parts of him were discovered.

'Unfortunately, I could not follow in his footsteps,' continued his father. 'But you are smart. You have potential. You can go to IIT. You can be a great engineer like him.'

Kaizad said nothing. The careers he visualised veered between becoming a Test cricketer or Formula 1 driver.

After dinner, he watched Chhota Bheem on TV and went to bed. He could hear Tai washing dishes downstairs and murmurs of his parents conversing. 'We can't afford to spend a bomb on Kaizad's tuitions,' Mother was saying.

'Don't economise on education,' replied Father. 'Cut luxuries, not essentials. We'll have more money once we move into a flat after the house gets sold.'

'What luxuries....?' scoffed Mother. 'We hardly see one movie a month. Tuitions are not essential for Kaizad. He's well above average in class.'

'To get into IIT, Kaizad must get at least 98 per cent.'

'He's still in grade five!'

'Education is a long-term investment. An IIT graduate's starting salary is in lakhs.'

'What if he has other ideas?'

'He's a sensible boy. Always takes my guidance. Problem is he spends half his time dreaming.'

Kaizad fell asleep smiling. Practical Mother. Idealistic Father. Only adventure was missing from his life. So, he had to create it.

His dream of hiding inside the Trojan horse with Greek soldiers and slaughtering enemies was interrupted by horrendous caterwauling. He squashed a pillow over his ears. Sound penetrated. Moonlight touched a corner of his bed. Eyelids tingled under translucent light. He turned to face a three-quarter moon.

'Nothing like mating cats to disturb a night's sleep,' Father had grumbled while training the garden hose on the pair two nights ago. Tonight no one did anything. The crescendo continued. Cats sounding amazingly like babies. Groggily tottering to the window, Kaizad hurled a ball in the direction of the cacophony. A pause. A scuffle in the shrubbery. Then the wailing resumed.

The sky was awash with milky light. Rainbow-edged cloud clumps flirted with the moon. Kaizad watched them disintegrate and regroup into a headless horse, a stegosaurus with horns spitting fire, a bat with outstretched wings, the moon peeping out as an eye.

Yawning, he returned to bed, covering his head with a bed sheet to escape the moon's glowering gaze. Bluish light filtered through. With it an idea. A perfect time for a ghostly rehearsal. He sat up, aware it was well past midnight.

Indoors it was quiet, except for his Father's snores. If anyone had woken up to the caterwauling, they had, by now, returned to slumber land. White sheet and torch in hand, he crept towards the narrow stairs, jumping over the creaky third step to avoid making a sound. In a few moments, he was on the terrace.

The fused bulb had not been replaced. Kaizad fumbled in the dark, fingers tangling in cobwebs before closing over the box with his newfound treasures. Carrying it out into the moonlight, he opened it, once again startled by the grinning teeth. Chuckling at his nervousness, he started sticking the teeth onto the white sheet with long strips of tape.

The effect was not as ghostly as he had imagined. He contemplated the glasses. Cutting smaller strips of tape, Kaizad balanced the glasses at the right distance from the teeth. The tape did not hold the thin wire rim.

He cut longer strips, rolled the tape around each spectacle arm and stuck it on the sheet. The spectacles toppled. Try as he did, they refused to stand erect over the teeth. After the fifth attempt, Kaizad was ready to give up. The only thing to do was drape the sheet with dentures over himself, wear the glasses over it and emerge when Natasha was playing with her Barbie.

A dragon cloud sailed past, tail flicking moon-face. Moonlight remained milky bright. The caterwauling had subsided. Torch in hand, he got under the sheet, fingering the teeth over his mouth, balancing the glasses above them, carefully wedging each spectacle arm behind his ears. He wished he could see himself.

No broken mirror to show his reflection in this dusty room. Paint cans returned only a shadowy silhouette. Then Kaizad had an idea. Water would show his reflection.

Torch pointed at toes, he took a few steps towards the water tank. Hidden in the sheet, Kaizad could see neither terrace nor beyond its wall, only the odd shape of his feet on the steps and the floor below them.

Clutching the rim of the tank, he was about to lift its lid when an ear-shattering scream rent the air and a window in the neighbouring house slammed shut. Startled, Kaizad dropped his disguise, fled down the stairs and jumped into bed. That scream was loud enough to wake the dead, he thought, wondering what might have upset poor Mrs Shetty at this unearthly hour.

Tuning ears to his parents' bedroom, he listened for signs of them being awake. If they found him on the terrace at midnight, there'd be no football for a week. As rhythmic snores kept pace with the clock, he relaxed. All was well.

Early morning, he found a draught Mrs Shetty in agitated conversation with Father. Had she seen him? Was she complaining?

Father kept shaking his head, murmuring, 'That's not possible, Mrs Shetty, you must be dreaming.' Relieved, Kaizad gulped down breakfast and ran off to school from the kitchen exit.

'Why did Mrs Shetty come over this morning?' he asked Father that evening.

Father gave him a long look before answering, 'Son, you are now old enough to face skeletons in our family closet.' He led him towards the oil lamp with his grandfather's photograph. 'This here is my father. He died before you were born,' he said softly, as if Kaizad didn't know.

'I've told you your grandfather was brilliant. He was always fixing things around the house. We never had to call an electrician or plumber because he was Mr Fix-it, as your generation would say.

'That day he was on the terrace doing something with the water tanks. When he didn't come down, my mother sent me to call him. He was nowhere to be seen. Then I spotted the open lid and...his body...floating.... No one knows how he fell in...'

Eyes moist, his father's voice tailed off. Kaizad hadn't got an answer for Mrs Shetty's visit.

At dinner, Kaizad tried again. 'Dad, why did Mrs Shetty come so early today?'

This time his father gave a wan smile. 'She imagined she saw my father's ghost at the water tank.'

Kaizad went into peals of laughter. 'Ghost…. She saw a ghost! I thought only Natasha was scared of ghosts….!'

'Even adults can be irrational, son.'

'So stupid, Dad, couldn't she see it was me!'

'You!' Laughter died as both parents looked at him aghast.

Reluctantly, he nodded, 'I was only fooling…'

'At 2 am?'

'The cats woke me up… I couldn't go back to sleep so ….'

'Why did Mrs Shetty think you were a ghost?'

'I was practising…to frighten Natasha…dressing in a sheet…' Kaizad sensed he was in serious trouble. 'And dentures…' he finished lamely.

'Dentures! Where did you find dentures?'

'In th…the…box…upstairs…' he managed to stammer.

Mother was looking as pale as the sheet he had dressed up in. 'Mrs Shetty has told everyone our house is haunted with Pappa's ghost. We'll never be able to sell it now.'

Father ignored her. 'Why were you climbing on the tank?'

'To see my reflection in the water,' he mumbled.

And Kaizad received the first stinging slap from Father.

The Dance of the Happy Muse

Rinita Banerjee

I am at the museum.

Amid the hum and quiet of many a human voice, their footsteps on the museum floors like leisurely raindrops on wet earth, I stand facing Marie Genevieve van Goethem. Made of beeswax, clay and metal armature, Edgar Degas's *Little Dancer Aged Fourteen* stands enclosed in a speckless glass embrace, dressed in a cotton faille bodice, cotton and silk tutu, and linen slippers, her hair tied in a beige-coloured silk and linen ribbon. It is the original wax sculpture that Degas had first exhibited in Paris back in 1881, the exhibition brochure in my hand reveals. Although surrounded on the walls with other framed proofs, in chalk, pastel and oil, of the artist's deft hands, his heedful, obsessive eyes and, through them, detailed glimpses of ballerinas' lives behind the stage, when they weren't tiptoeing themselves to become music that breathed, there is this—once-body, now-not—that enwreathes me in a contemplative mist.

The phone buzzes in my trouser pocket, the vibration piercing my skin like the blunt claws of some insect, struggling relentlessly to tear through the sleepy cotton fabric. I am acutely aware that this is the sixth time the phone has rung since I entered the museum, and I haven't answered it.

I continue to stand, immobile, my head tilted slightly to my right, arms across my chest, staring at Marie. Staring at it meant not looking at the phone screen meant not seeing who was calling meant not being obligated to respond, not for once, not now, not now, not for some time more, some more time.

11:55 am. It isn't time yet for me to be back. Lunch won't be this soon. I am away, on a tour of the museum. I am away, I am all right, I am not thinking beyond what lies immediately in front of me—a piece of art as immobile as myself. I am just seeing, observing, thinking and breathing—air. Air, air, air—I *see* it too.

Next in my line of sight is another figure. Not made of wax, metal, wood or plastic. She arrives between me and Marie, seats herself on the rectangular marble seat, her back towards me. By the time I am aware of her presence, she has already turned her face—I haven't been able to see it— towards the sculpture.

There have been others who have stood awhile and left, unlike me, who remains standing and watching the statuette—her head thrust back, chin turned upwards, arms stretched to the back, the fingers interlocked, eyes half-closed, standing on a wooden plank with her right foot placed forward, toes turned a sharp right, her left foot behind, toes pointing slightly diagonally to the left. It must have been painful, tedious, even boring to pose like that, for hours, day after day, and it took Degas four years to complete this sculpture. My mother once told me that he did not really care much for ballet, let alone the ballerinas, *les petits rats*, as these girls in the corps de ballet at the Paris Opera were called in those days. It was habitual of her to know all about the artists whose works she was fond of. One of mother's favourite Degas paintings was the *Blue Dancers*. 'The artist's interest lay not so much in portraying the ballerinas as fairies sprinkling stardust on the watchers' hearts, but in capturing the dancers' realities offstage,' I think, she said. And so, in his paintings, we have the ballet dancers rehearsing on stage, at the foyer, them hard at work at the barre. I had read in an article sometime back—it was on a book written about this little dancer—that a year after the completion of this sculpture, Marie was dismissed from the Paris Opera on account of being late to class on several occasions. Her posing for Degas apparently being the reason behind the lateness. She was an artist's model also training to be a ballerina. It was difficult to trace her after that, the article had mentioned. Where did she go? I, too, wonder about that today, especially today. I have not reached her story yet. Make no mistake though. I am no hunter for such truths. The contemplation only allows a purpose to be fulfilled—to leave my story behind, for some time more, some more time. Marie, therefore, is my muse too, you see. I am no artist though. Make no mistake. But it is because of her, after all, that I see air. In fact, seeing the position of the head, I ponder if Marie, too, wasn't attempting to breathe through the smell of paint, pigmented beeswax and clay that would have pervaded the artist's chamber in which she was his muse. If she, too, wasn't in search of air. Did she find it?

This woman who sits a few steps ahead of me—her hair, thick, black, ends just above the nape of her neck. It covers a head that is oval, fully. Fully oval, that is. As she stares ahead, her head tilted to the right, too, I notice how her body sits still, not a trace of the tides of breath. A cloth bag, a lovely amber in colour, with not a crease on it, almost as if it had been ironed, rests between her left hand and waist. Her elbows are like round stains of rouge on milk-white cheeks; against the black, sleeveless, knee-length dress, they stand out even more. She is thin. The V of her dress on the back lets me see the interlocking bones on her spinal column, almost pushing through the glowing skin.

She, too, regards Marie. What else is there to see ahead of her? Air? Could she, too, see air? Wish I could find out.

The insect had awoken again. A seventh time.

I am not letting it out. It is no firefly in a glass jar. It won't fly away. I won't pursue its glow to anywhere. It will usurp air. Gladly dethrone me from the seat of breather. Gluttonous, wretched insect. I am not going to let it out.

I want to see her face. I feel a sudden urge to do so. I want to sit beside her. The urge is overtaking me. Maybe, after some time, even talk to her? About air, among other things? I take the first step, but even before the foot can touch the polished museum floor, I stop and consider putting ahead my right toe first instead. En pointe. I will rest my body on the ball of my foot, one foot at a time. I will tiptoe towards this woman in black and amber and pink and white and flesh and muscle and bones and blood. I am all warmed up, a ballerina. This, a game of *as if*. And she, the woman, is Marie, returning to tell her story, *as if*. We are not stuck inside frames and glass boxes, no longer prey to light and colour and paints.

Prêt pour la danse.

How Marie continues to be my muse! Me, now author of this fantasia. Artist me. So soon, the becoming. It gladdens my heart. I smile.

No sooner does *la danse* begin, something happens. As I tiptoe towards Marie-*as if*, hardly succeeding in keeping my balance for even over half a second on the ball of my foot, my strides unhurried, I notice a soft movement on her part. She has dived into that amber cloth bag of hers and has taken something out. I cannot see what. Her head is still fixed on the statuette in front of her though. A few seconds pass. I am closing in on her. Seconds more, and I see her body assume less taut a stance. There is almost no one between us now, but something has happened. My stomach churns with a faint tremor. I shudder slightly. The music has reached a crescendo too quick. I must abandon my game. In a single long stride, I reach immediately behind her to find that she has cut her left wrist, made a clean cut with a small, sharp blade that appears to be a paper knife that she is holding in her right fist. My eyes on the hands, I still don't see her face. I so want to, but, somehow, I can't bring myself to do so. I don't hear her cry, although, by now, she must be sensing a dull throb, a niggling pain. Isn't that what it must feel like? It will soon be monstrous agony, baring its teeth, sharp shards of glass hungry for flesh, for life, too, maybe. *La danse*—of death? Has it just begun? How did we reach the end so quickly?

I must hold her, call someone, but neither my hands nor my voice move. Seconds more pass, maybe minutes, I can't count. Meanwhile, her body tilts slowly to her left, her head slumps forward, but before she can fall, limp from the blood loss, I catch her, screaming, 'Help! Help!' I must have articulated that word several times emptily before it met the sound, the noise, the scream, the wail oozing from my voice box, for my mouth feels weary from some kind of weight, of being agape too long. People begin to trickle around me, gathering like the blood dropping from her wrist on to the museum floor. I see the shock on their faces. I see a museum security guard mouthing something into his radio transceiver. They take hold of her. I have left her in their hands. Even when I held her, I kept my distance. How strange, this sudden compulsion of mine to separate myself from her, away, further. From her, from her death, from death. Some kind of end—mine, of me?

So many questions race through my mind: Why did she have to take her life? That too at a museum? Particularly here? In front of Marie? Why at all?

My ears close themselves to the gasps, the urgency in the voices around me, except that I hear the buzz of the insect in my trouser pocket. It has risen again, its incessant gnawing, in loops of exactly a minute each, reminds me of my story, no longer hidden behind the haze of make-believe. It's time to return.

I have been found. Found out. I don't remain lost. Unlike Marie.

Besides, Marie need no longer be my muse.

I see air no more. There's no more air to see.

I pull out my phone, order a cab on Uber and hasten myself out of the museum. I abandon the images of what transpired inside, like I would sweep thick dust from atop an old glass table with a cloth. What would be left on it would soon be motes in the air, spittle, anonymous, outside, away, further. I must not care, not now, not now, not for a long time to come.

Once inside the cab, I concentrate on the phone screen. The call log shows 10 missed calls: Mou Pishi, Mou Pishi, Baba, Baba, Baba, Baba, Baba, Baba, Baba, Baba. I am saved from the memory of a body losing life in my hands, the sickening lull of an impending end, of silence grasping my vocal cords, of the fear I felt by how close she was to me. Plague—*as if*. *La danse*—*c'est finis*—*as if*. A pirouette gone wrong, an ankle snapped while on en pointe—*as if*. Curtains—*as if*.

Baba, Baba, Mou Pishi, Mou Pishi, Mou Pishi, Baba—six more missed calls. I do not respond. There is nothing to say. I cannot bring home grief. It is where I live.

I am home.

'*Ei toh, Suro eshey gaechey!*' says Mou Pishi as she opens the door of her house to let me in. 'Where have you been, Suro?

We have been trying your phone since the last two hours! Where have you been?' I can almost see the frown in her voice. I don't look at her face.

'I was at the museum. I thought we were on a holiday here,' I say calmly while removing my shoes, my eyes towards the floor. I am trying very hard not to let exasperation take over.

'Oh, but why didn't you say anything? You could have simply picked up the phone and said you were at the museum. You know how your Baba gets without you...'

'Where had you gone off to, Suro? I woke up to see you weren't home...' says Baba, coming up to me.

I pour myself a glass of water. 'They had an exhibition of Degas's paintings, Baba. Remember how Ma used to...'

'You weren't home, I was so worried. Why did you go without telling me? Without telling Pishi ... I called you so many times...'

'Ma had framed cut-outs of Degas's paintings from a wall calendar Pishi had sent her from here ... remember? She was very fond of his works...'

'Where is your phone? Show me, show me...' I realise Baba wasn't listening to me. I look at my father, let out a sigh, and taking my phone out of my trouser pocket, hand it over to him.

'Sixteen missed calls! Do you see, do you?' Baba almost shouts, his voice slightly tremulous. 'I didn't even have my lunch, and I am hungry.' Baba's voice now wears a muffled garb.

Although I stare at the carpeted floor, I can see the tears gathering along the rims of my seventy-two-year-old father's eyes. They will soon swarm past the broken skin of his cheeks.

'I did not want to have lunch without you. I never do. Your mother always ate her lunch with me until she....'

Mou Pishi, my father's only sister, whom Baba and I have come to visit in Washington DC, stands silently by the sofa I now sit on. My arms across my chest and eyes still fixed on the floor, I feel her eyes on me. I have resigned to Baba's tears. I let them flow. There is nothing to say.

I must be there when Baba has his meals. Twice a day. A ritual he never lets go of since my mother passed away—it's been a year. A ritual I cannot turn my back to, so complete in the knowledge that he can't bear being on his own, and despite being so certain of the knowledge that he cannot reach the loneliness I suffer—*that I, too, suffer*—yet must embody, each day. He and I aren't the same, yet we are.

While he can never be whole despite my presence, I can never be whole despite his. I know it all from both ends. He refuses the knowledge altogether.

I must be there, be there, be there, like he says he was when I was growing up. Be there, be there, be there.

I cannot be lost.

I cannot be dead.

I *must* be there.

I cannot see air.

Baba does not shout any more. I hear him snivel. I still don't look at him. I suddenly feel Mou Pishi's hand on my head, almost like my mother's. I want to reach that warmth, drown my face into its depths and cry, for hours, until I can cry no more, see no more, hear no more, smell no more, feel no more. I know she knows the abyss that is my helplessness, but she can never say it. I can't either. I drink the tears that pool in my throat, shove them down as much as I can.

'Come, let's have lunch. I have made your favourite mutton kosha,' says Mou Pishi. A pause, and then she adds, 'It's the recipe Boudi taught me. I even garnished it with some fried onions. You will like it. Come, Suro. Dada, come on … Now Suro has returned, come, let's eat…'

Pishi waits some more, her hand gently stroking my head until it stops. She heads towards the table. I don't look at her.

The woman in black and amber and pink and white and flesh and muscle and bones and blood. Not Marie. I know she isn't her.

I am playing no longer.

Did she die? If she did, a passing I shall never know the reason behind, such peace she must feel. Did anyone call her? How many calls might she have missed? Did she see me while I dreaded to look beyond the blood? I wish she saw me and knew I was there, just behind her, keen to know her story. How alone she must have been. Had it blinded her so she could no longer dream of seeing air? But, the dread… What was I so afraid to see?

And Marie? I wish I could ask her if she ever knew air. But would she tell me? Wasn't I glad to make her my muse? Like my father makes of me? Marie—subject to an artist's creation. To me, once-auteur—a means to a fantasia obfuscating my reality. In a game, a pawn. Merely that. But, am I any different? Perhaps. I am the perfect son to his father. Yes, oh yes. A *happy* muse then? Euphemism.

Marie laughs, somewhere. The mirror in front of her, reflects me. Me, wearing the face I couldn't bear to see at the museum. Or is it? I am not certain of even that.

I, Sourith Bose, son of Sourjendu Bose—found out.

Gluttonous, wretched insect—I let it out. It won.

Make no mistake, it won.

Prêt pour la danse?

Honour

Rochelle Potkar

White clothes had to be washed separately, and that was the catch. It was the shirts' problem if they stained. A soak, a bleach, a rinse, a double dose of detergent, more time in the sun. If the stains didn't go, there were chances Purna would have to pay for the shirt, which would be discarded by the owner and come to her.

Even now she wore an old shirt over her sari—the first remembrance of carelessness that she paid for with her entire month's earnings, years ago. It had the spoils of pink colour over the horizons of the yoke and hem, like the new sun enveloping rouge clouds at 6 am, glazing the concrete citadel of drying clothes in red, blue, white and green amid its grey cubicles.

As the city moved around, marking the beginning of another day in four square directions, it seemed to hold Purna at the centre—arms twisted, fabric gripping wet, her body taut, thrashing out the garment over the flogging stone in one sweep—removing city grime and sweat from two thick saris.

Purna stopped to look at the cars at the traffic lights as a train rattled on the other side from Mahalaxmi station. Sometimes she wondered about those cars. What if someone was watching through darkened windows? What if they knew what she was up to? Those people with books on their laps...

But she did not stop. Like the hands of a clock, she wound her seasoned arm-swings around the stone until noon, chasing detergent from linen.

When she was done, she bought a plate of rice, roti, dal and sabzi from the dhobis who cooked at the ghat. She ate and quickly headed home to cook for Pakya, packing his food in a tiffin and dropping it off at the jail. Whoever ate it, if he didn't, could go to hell.

She got back to the ghat at 3 pm, and until 8, raced with the setting sun and the emerging moon to wrap up her work, pull clothes off entwined ropes where they had dried under the noon's crispness. She hurried to iron, fold, code and bundle them into a sheet. Someone loaded that onto her back.

When she crossed the late-night signal, she peered through car windows again, searching those faces. Someone in there behind the glinting glasses surely knew.

She remembered her father beating their mother in her growing-up days. Those never-ending drunken, yelling nights. Her sister Anju, brother Pakya, huddled in a dark corner—sleepy but shivering in the humidity.

It was not surprising then that she disbelieved in marriage. At 26, all she wanted was to stand on her feet—even if they were itchy from the water, soaked in chemicals, soda, solvents, detergent, bleach and whiteners. First, her feet got soft. The thick skin peeled. Then, the thin skin. Her feet looked misshapen like candle wax. She watched them, now barefoot, trampling over the dark mud of Bombay.

She had only one pair of slippers that she wore on customer rounds. She appeared quiet to them with her topaz nose-ring that spoke more in the sheen of the light than her.

As she untied sacks, gracefully handing ironed shirts, trousers, saris to customers, she pulled off the tag with the inked codes, relieved of her responsibility. Then, she headed to the next house.

She knew some of her customers from Baba Adam's age. And on their part, they had made their impressions of her. Some thought she was too proud and educated because she scribbled the accounts in English with a blue refill that she dug out of her blouse or from her ponytail's scrunchy.

Purna had studied up to the 10th standard. That's when their father had absconded. Anju got pregnant and had to be married off, and overnight she took to running the house. Their mother ailed in grief, heartbreak and hopelessness in a corner; she stopped praying to the gods kept in the bare wooden frame.

No wonder it wasn't important to possess a husband as much as savings so if she married, she would have the money to leave behind a troublesome man. That is what one needed. Life insurance against a man. Husband-protection. Gone were the days of sewing-embroidering, housekeeping and cooking. Now it was time to wield a knife (not just to chop onions), a stick behind the kitchen door for emergencies and jewellery for pawning for sudden money needs.

Pakya had turned out to be an impressionable bastard, then a vagrant.

Now everywhere she went, she had to deal with it. Shameful words spreading...

All the customers spoke about him. To her—she, who had never spoken about herself. Now they knew he had raped and killed a girl. And that the girl was 16. And Pakya had stalked her. And when she was alone, barged into her house, into the dank weirdness of his own darkness.

Because the girl had screamed and retaliated, it had gone really bad. Pakya had battered her, after she hit his head with something heavy. He killed her. Once rage enters a person... it intermingles with fear. She knew that from her father. She knew that of herself.

Then the bastard had absconded, with a commingling of blood on his clothes—of his, of the girl's—and so many eyewitnesses around. He was caught by the police, taken into custody and hammered to a pulp every day.

Now that he was in jail, their mother nagged Purna to go meet him. There was always love mixed with regret, mixed with dependence.

'We cannot ignore him,' her mother said in a scratchy, coughing voice, 'Go meet him. Take some food for him.'

And so, after delivering ironed clothes the next week, Purna collected dirty linen, made a jaunt to the ghat, washed, ironed and made a dash to jail.

She avoided Pakya's gaze. They had beaten him up so that his face was purple and swollen. 'Very good,' she mumbled. 'You are turning out like father. How could you…?'

But if that wasn't enough, Pakya was now on TV. All her customers, dhobis and *dhoban*s from the ghat, the neighbours knew about him. They would ask her:

Did he really do it?

Was he in love with that girl?

Will he be released?

When will he be released?

When is the hearing?

Is the verdict out?

Is he your real brother?

Did you always know he was a rapist?

Her peace shattered, her plans for the future turned dim. Each day carrying clothes up and down seemed like a mammoth task. Many a time, she dumped her bundles to the side of the road, squatted and wailed.

She felt the itch on her feet as she deposited the last of the clothes to the customer.

The next day, she left all her bundles by the house door. She spent hours cooking and using up all the spice from the paper packet. Her mother tossed and turned in bed. 'Is today a feast or someone's birthday? *Sevai*? *Kheer*? *Biryani*? I want to eat today, even if I vomit.'

So, she kept food for Mother and then headed out.

In the night, when she returned, news of Pakya's death had reached everywhere like dirty foamy brine draining off a cubicle floor.

They would come for her. Somebody from the city.

On the shaky TV, she watched the news at 10. Yesterday, it was about an acid attack. Today, about a couple who were hacked to death for marrying outside their caste.

Pakya had to have a post-mortem done on him.

She went back to the jail and cried. She blamed the police for sabotage. She wailed and protested, making herself unreasonable. They shushed her and asked her to go.

She let Pakya go.

They may have been poor, but their family name had improved after their father's disappearance, up until now.

Slowly, the questions stopped coming in. She stopped squatting on the margins of the road. Who really cared for the death or the murder of a rapist?

Today foreigners hanging around the parapet descended to click pictures. She did not look at them, but her heart beat like torrential rain on tin roofs. They pointed their cameras as she swung thick curtains on the stone. In a betrayal of what she had no name for, they zoomed out their elephant-trunk-like lens to her face and splashed light on her. She scrunched her face and continued working.

Clean, well-ironed linen delivered on time was all the world wanted.

Now with the TV set in grey silence like a toy without its battery or key, Purna ran her hands over her shins that bore permanent purple marks from bumping over different stones all these years at the ghat.

Some stains would never go away, with any ointment, *malham* or *lape*.

Marietta's Song

Sarah Robertson

The paper mill at the bottom of the hill was an asylum before an old folk's home. And it was when I went to work there that I learned to believe in miracles.

'The insanity still seeps from the brickwork,' shrieked Pippa Small in her Yorkshire drawl when things went wrong, and that was often. The rosacea-faced former nurse often said the home was cursed, and she wasn't liked by many of her wealthy wards. They eyed her with suspicion and surprise as she waddled around blinking her bloodshot bleary eyes. She looked like she didn't sleep properly and that she slyly dipped her hand into her own medicine trolley.

The paddles on the mill's wheel continued to turn, their splashing repetition a type of therapy for many who were no longer able to recall which world they were in or where they'd come from. Mrs McConnally with the colostomy had all her faculties still. She had a faint grin even when we were thin on the ground with much-needed nurses. Mr Kleimer had grade-four Alzheimer's and couldn't manage a single sentence. He chuntered on, his nonsensical din vaguely amusing kind carers. Their rooms were magnificent, with dramatic views of the river Trent and over a series of capacious man-made waterfalls. The mill sat on a lip of the wide river that divided briefly to deliver its load to the ever-hungry, interminable turning wheel.

The stream of rich old dears came from very far and very near, their deep blue veins pulsing through delicate paper-thin skin, surfacing uncomfortably like Ms Small's disdain. She left food out of reach and call bells unanswered, pressure sores deep and patients with cancer scratching around without medication, a shortage of nurses to do a rotation.

It was a dreary rainy Tuesday when Norwegian Marietta came to stay. Long-limbed, lean, thin and baby blonde hair, she could have pretended to be an ABBA member if she'd cared.

'Totally bonkers,' Pippa said about our latest resident with dementia.

'Bloody fruitloop,' she needlessly spat as she hammered a calculator with her fat sausage finger, totting up her bulky monthly income with the grit and greed of an evil ruler in a very, very, very, very tiny kingdom. She was someone I desperately wanted to stay away from. Of course, I was able to go back home at the end of the day. Free to some extent, in my own way. Away from the ever-hungry, interminable turning wheel. Home to the sanity of a kitchen fire, the dog chewing a sock, the blackbird on the windowsill, the reassuring bass tick of the grandfather clock.

'Read her this,' Pip mumbled at me as she checked her Facebook page. 'And get used to it,' she continued, 'The mentalist wants it every day.'

I held three sheets of crisp A4, across them a story. About two lovers who had met aboard a boat called 'Royaltide Glory'.

'Her memory notes?' I asked, perplexed, as Pip updated her status.

And I considered how the tool I clutched could be an apparatus. To help our Norwegian friend recall her life, her love, her heart. As the dusty books on the shelves of her fragile memory slowly fell apart. Like rotting leaves swept away and carried by the wind. Spinning in ever-decreasing circles like a dirty, discarded lemon-rind-coloured window blind.

'It's not true,' snorted Nurse Belleview, pointing at the pages uncannily.

'She was already gone when she wrote that song. It's nothing short of pure fantasy.'

The ironically named nurse Belleview was Pip's right-hand woman. And I knew when a crowd wasn't a team, what I should say and what I shouldn't. I nodded and smiled, remaining dry-eyed, but inside a hopeful part of me died.

And the paddles on the mill's wheel continued to turn.

Marietta was ill before it distilled, not immediately evident to her family. She kept getting lost in familiar places and couldn't get home. Oh, such agony! A doctor neighbour found her one day, standing confused in the corner shop. She was wearing ten watches on each arm, each set to different times, a different face on each different desperate but inaccurate clock.

So, I read the story to our Miss Norway, gladly leading the way. To a beautiful place for Marietta to grace, a passageway back to her memories.

For months, we journeyed, every night. Marietta and me, we were birds without flight, looking down onto a beautiful world where two lovers let their passion unfold.

She was only 20 when, in her bikini, she gripped the side of the yacht with her toes, the salty spray spitting coolly across her letterbox-red nails.

It was a world of privilege, a stuffy delight, pre-dinner martinis every night. Afternoon tea on the royal deck, where men in starched uniforms kept check. One in particular chased her down, a curious man with a foppish frown.

Apologetically, curiously shy despite being directly tied to the throne of the British Empire. And because of this they had to conspire. To keep their affair completely out of sight. Worn only through the night, the sapphire ring, the diamond necklace. Oh, so much bling over champagne breakfasts! 'He has a girlfriend,' her friend hissed. 'You're totally reckless. Her name's Camilla, and she's very well-connected.'

'That's what they do these men. They'll pick you up then drop you. You're nothing but a fleeting whim, a floating piece of jetsam.'

'He didn't though,' Marietta said, with clarity and nonchalance, as she brushed a piece of fluff from her t-shirt front.

'You'll see,' she said. 'It's quite a thing. It's my birthday tomorrow. He never forgets like us old gits. He'll bring me a song at up-tempo.

It was here I started to steer towards my own worried mind. How would she feel when Mr Royal didn't appear, or was I unkind? Would she forget this passing kismet she'd created as a distraction, or would she remember to be disappointed when her own fiction didn't happen?

Tomorrow came, and I was ready early at the desk. 'I may as well take reception,' I chirpily protest. 'Linda deserves a break, and well, my legs are bad. I fell walking the dog at dawn and I feel I may expire.'

Pippa smirked the way she did, a smile just on one side. She often looked as if she'd had a stroke then she'd died. 'If we're working you too hard, you know you can just say, the Job Centre's merely a hop skip jump away.'

All day I spent with pent-up angst, watching the front door as rain stained the window pane with bubbles and leaves from the Sycamore. We'd had 15 visitors, including a Labrador, by the time the clock struck five. Oh my, was Marietta not cared for? I'd never locked a door with such a laden heart, and as I felt Marietta's dream tumble apart, a leather-gloved hand tapped the thin glass window pane, in a dancing rhythm in a way that entertained. It was like a highland fling, a ceilidh on the trot, a super Alabama slide, an American foxtrot. I clicked and snapped the shutter open. In the dark, a man stood hopeful, gleaming eyes, his chest was lifted, chin was raised.

'I have a gift for Madam M Kristofferson. The lady Scandinavian. I am here by royal decree that guarantees delivery of Marietta's birthday song. My master pays the fees you see, it's in your contract that annually I will come to play and play to wash the opaque clouds away.'

He strode across the hall as if he knew where he was going, straight into the living room, his sense of duty bursting. The black lid of the piano lifted, he sunk his fingers into a gift of magic notes of a magic song, enough to lift the dead along into a world of passionate flight, with pre-dinner martinis every night. Afternoon tea on the royal deck, where love eternal spans bedecked, refusing to be contained by the treachery of amnesic waves.

As I felt my skin prickle, I noticed at the open window a man whose face I recognised, but not just from Marietta's lines. He was standing in the shadow, letting his eyes drink her in, taking in the magic he had never stopped believing in.

It was Marietta's song, and as she sang, it became clear she'd known it all along. Her lost chords weren't in the past, her explosive dreams had hatched. No one in that stunned audience had known that she could sing. Her voice was celestial, an operatic trill. The notes they hung together, sliding and yet still. The memory of a thousand pleasures suspended in that mill.

I went home to the kitchen fire, the dog still chewing a sock, the blackbird on the windowsill and the bass tick of the grandfather clock. I thought of how she'd shone, from where she'd come and what he'd done.

And of how Marietta's song had let me believe in love.

The Vacation

Shilpa Raina

The sound of her husband's cough broke the stillness of the night and yanked her out of sleep. Her eyes met the darkness the room was filled with. It wasn't unusual. She quickly moved her right hand to locate the torch. As she switched it on to scan the face of her husband, she saw that he faced the wall where the clock rested. He appeared comfortable though. She then trained it on the clock: 3 am. She wasn't sure when she fell asleep. Or whether she slept at all. Her eyelids felt heavy. But what she remembered clearly was lying next to him. On his right side, as always. But worried and anxious, looking outside through the window, reminiscing about their lives, their decades of togetherness. And uncertainties tomorrow would bring. When and how she succumbed to sleep, she couldn't recollect. But this was, perhaps, the first time in many years they had slept on the same bed without engaging in a pre-bedtime conversation—a pattern that had developed on its own after their children moved to bigger cities for a better life.

The 37 years of marriage had perfected their negotiating skills to tolerate each other's idiosyncrasies. A sense of familiarity about each other's imperfections had also dissipated the idea of a perfect marriage. That was why the flickering embers of their fights no more made to the bedroom. Or, perhaps, they had realised that with just two of them, a quarrel would further add to the ominous silence— an uneasy quietude none of them wanted in the house. With their children away, reconciliation proved to be the best antidote to avoid unnecessary discord. Her mind was preoccupied with these thoughts before sleep engulfed her. The assessment of the contours of their relationship even surprised her, as she never had the time to analyse their bond. Introspection was never her forte. But tonight was different because never before has she been in such a situation.

Her reverie was broken by another cough. This time, a loud one. She got up and switched on the light only to find that her husband had vomited the milk he drank before he went to sleep. The white, foamy liquid had soiled the cushion and his side of the bed. She panicked, her mind froze. But then she collected herself and decided to first take him to the washroom. As she helped him get up from the bed, he struggled to even sit still. His body wobbled and the head slipped to the left. With her petite frame, it was not easy to manage his 72-kilogram body. Yet, she supported his unsteady body to help him get up. As he dragged his feet, she realised that the right side of his body was immobile— numb, listless, lifeless. With great difficulty, she first took him to the bathroom to clear his system and then helped him sit down on a brown plastic chair adjacent to the bed.

She then cleaned the bed, and changed the bed sheet and the cushion cover. Once again, she lifted his heavy body up from the chair, by holding his powerless right hand with all the strength she could summon. Talking one step at a time, she carefully laid him on the bed. As she sat next to him with a growing feeling of trepidation, she let her fingers slip through his thin hair, the tip of her fingers touching his scalp. Her cold fingers felt the currents of blood gushing through his head and the movement of life beneath it.

A wave of exhaustion had swept through her body. More than feeling tired, she was seized by a severe bout of fear. Of loneliness and dependency. She hadn't envisioned, until this moment, how her life would be without him. Deep down she knew it would be purposeless if he weren't around, though she had never publicly admitted her fears. There was never a need to do so either. After all, they both looked healthy. But then this happened: a clot in his head, and within 24 hours, she witnessed his slow and steady collapse, which began with him limping and ended with him being in a semi-conscious state.

An uninterrupted flow of distant relatives and neighbours had kept her busy during the day as they indefinitely parked themselves in different rooms of the house to 'discuss and debate' the next course of action. Deep-rooted patriarchy was on display. The decision-makers, obviously, were men. They all had suggestions to make on her behalf. They didn't even discuss the matter with their children, for they believed they were too young to decide. No one even bothered to ask her what she wanted. Perhaps, they had already presumed that she wouldn't know. For a woman, whose life mostly revolved around her children and household chores, the tag of 'homemaker' didn't qualify her as a 'decision-maker'.

The flow of nonsensical conversations had continued unabated throughout the day, with the concerned gentry discussing a range of subjects—from the appalling state of healthcare infrastructure to private hospitals mired in corruption. The single-storey structure had come alive with non-stop chatter, but the man of the house seemed to be fading away. Only a handful of folks appeared to be really concerned. The rest, to say the least, were audiences for an experiential event that would teach them a life lesson—how to prepare for health emergencies.

They finally reached a decision at 9:15 pm, and the children were informed and asked to book early morning tickets. Their flight was scheduled at 7 am.

In her 59 years of life, she had travelled on an airplane only once. That too for attending a family emergency. This was her second time. It was no coincidence that she opted for the 'expensive' mode of travel only during a crisis. Not that the family couldn't afford it. But after having been thrown into a life in penury, not once but twice, she feared being crushed by it again. It had also made her cautious of the truth that a financial tragedy might befall a third time too. Even though periods of misfortune taught her an important life skill—to compromise—it also instilled in her an irreversible sense of insecurity, which eventually guided her actions. As the shadows of those gloomy days refused to leave her, or was it the other way round, she learnt to survive. But then, she also forgot to live. Her husband and children—a daughter and a son—noticed her transformation from being joyous person to a worrisome one. But they weren't surprised. For they understood how she had braved grim circumstances that had disturbed the tranquillity of their lives. But what bothered them most was the onerous phase that had turned her into a cold miser. Surprisingly, not to their needs. But to her desires.

She heaved a sigh of relief when she sat next to her husband in the front row of the economy class in the aircraft. The first hurdle of passing through a series of security checks was smooth: no one noticed the man on the wheelchair in a semi-vegetative state providing a fillip to her confidence. But chances of being disembarked still loomed large, if any of the flight attendants got a whiff of her husband's precarious health condition. For no airline wants to run the risk of attending medical emergency thousands of feet above the ground. So, until the plane took off from the tier-II Indian city, she negotiated another bout of anxiety. It had become a discernible characteristic of her mind, shrouded with unwarranted thoughts and silent chatter like a long-playing gramophone record. It was not her fault though, as one-third of her life was spent in unending struggles that drilled into worries, anxiousness and fear. Her mind didn't know what else to do than to be on tenterhooks. But this time her anxiety was justifiable. She looked at her husband, whose head was covered in a woollen cap, to check if he was still breathing. With his sinking body camouflaged in a blanket, the only visible part was his face. And the only noticeable movement on his body—the quivering lips. The flight was yet to take off when a flight attendant came towards her. Her heart sank. The attendant looked at her husband suspiciously and enquired if everything was all right.

'Yes, we are going for a regular check-up. It is a routine. He is sleeping,' her confident voice belied the tempest engulfing her mind. The attendant didn't look convinced.

'Are you sure, ma'am?'

'Of course, why would I lie? And, most importantly, why would I risk his life? I am his wife, after all.'

'Umm… apologies, ma'am… it was just that he didn't look well. I wanted to ensure that any sort of emergency didn't cause inconvenience to our passengers. We are known for our service and punctuality.'

'I understand,' she said curtly.

Until the plane took off, she remained startled by her conduct with the air hostess. During the entire conversation, she had felt like a criminal who didn't want to surrender until proven guilty.

Any sign of timorousness or frailty would have flagged the flight attendant. But she had defended the lie with such fervent conviction that even rocks of truth melted under its heat. In that moment of trepidation, she had unlocked cavernous recesses of her soul where laid hidden scads of strength she didn't know existed. She had always displayed indefatigable resilience against the travesties of life, but the discovery about her courageous demeanour had befuddled her. For she had always played the second fiddle to her sisters, husband and even children. So, when she stood ground against the air hostess, with an unwavering commitment to her husband, Mrs Kaul was reminded of the heydays when confidence was the primary anchor of her life. The realisation that life wasn't bereft of the essential tool and it still existed within her brought a smile on her lips. She took a deep breath, closed her eyes, put her right hand around her husband's left arm and told herself things will be fine. This time too.

Everything looked hazy when he opened his eyes. The first thing he noticed was the ceiling. It was white. He instantly knew it wasn't his house where the ceiling was embellished with a brownish PVC sheet. In a state of grogginess, he tried to move his right hand but couldn't. He could feel layers of bandage around his head. Something went wrong, he thought. Much as he strained his brain to trace the residues of latest memory, it failed him. As the whitewashed walls stared back at him, Mr Kaul realised he has survived to hear the story.

In the main hall of the hospital building, which housed multiple operation theatres, she had seated herself on one of the three-seater aluminium chairs. The handbag, made from an old fuchsia sari, clutched close to her chest. As she pretended to watch the world go by, her mind took a deep dive to retrieve painful memories that had refused to heal. Around 23 years ago, she had stuffed her bags as hurriedly and haphazardly as she had done the night before. Yet, not picking anything randomly. It was incredible how her mind worked faster during a crisis. She had realised it first when, around two decades ago, she was escorted by local policemen to her house in Srinagar to pack essentials as fast as she could so that they could leave the precinct, vulnerable to attacks by terrorists, safely. After all, it was outside her own house her father-in-law laid in a pool of blood a day before. The family couldn't even grieve properly, for they feared for their safety. Such toxic was the insuperable wave of insurgency in the early 1990s in India's cradle of syncretism—Kashmir—that the life of a Pandit was not even worth a penny. So, when the floodgates of indiscriminate persecution opened, all that Kashmiri Pandits could do was to run. And her family, too, was running for their lives. She had arrived alone in the house, making decisions on behalf of the joint family. She felt the weight of responsibilities burdening her shoulders. As the eldest daughter-in-law, her time of reckoning had finally arrived in a joint family set-up. With a sensible approach, she had then begun packing. And despite restrictions on the number of baggage she could carry, she had managed to bring the cooking gas cylinder, for she knew that food was an absolute necessity for survival. Though later, when her husband questioned the rationale behind the selection of what he thought were inessential items, the cylinder turned out to be one of the most useful possessions among the list of useless objects.

The new life awaiting them in a different city was no less than a punishment. Here, the scourge of living in makeshift camps was compounded by fewer job opportunities and a never-ending struggle to assimilate. In times like these, every expense mattered. She became the custodian of balance sheets and meticulously recorded every transaction in her notebooks, as if maintaining a personal journal. The clerical job helped to keep the family afloat as she kept a hawkish control over the expenses. She perfectly understood the importance of thrift and saving. Slowly but steadily, they rebuilt their lives from dilapidation. A feeling of contentment prevailed alongside the pain of living in exile. But they somehow felt settled. Little knowing that their lives would be torpedoed, almost uprooting them once again.

It happened exactly after a decade. The sole breadwinner of the house, her husband, lost his job. For a man in his mid-40s, the prospect of finding a new job wasn't bright. They all knew it. But she was the most affected by this development. And this worry started creeping up on her. In the morass of financial hardships, the demons in her mind started whispering that she was useless. She began pinning the blame on herself for not being a 'working wife'. She was nothing but a burden on the family. Had she, too, been an earning member, they would have managed to oil the cogs of dwindling finances, she thought. The feeling of unworthiness made her wail. She pitied herself. And, eventually, she surrendered to her demonic voices. The only way to pay back, she thought, was by smothering her desires and needs. Which she skillfully did by dissembling herself, deliberately disliking things she once enjoyed. But her self-devised strategy wasn't enough to save the household from crumbling. So, she became edgy, with her mind overcast, numbed by a perpetual state of worry.

Most of the time, she behaved like a walking calculator, adding and subtracting numbers frantically to maintain balance in the ledger. Sometimes, she lost both her mind and sleep because of soaring inflation. She was inching closer to a nervous breakdown. But no one noticed. Somehow, she survived another bout of depression.

She sat still and dour, immune to the sounds and frantic activities around her, putting a figure to money that might be spent at the private hospital on her husband's treatment. Her heart shrank to the size of a pea when the estimated projection hinted at swallowing a major chunk of their savings of a lifetime. The thought that bits and pieces of her sacrifices would wither away with one unfortunate event had consumed her with a glowering sense of rage. Rather than celebrating life, she had chosen to mourn the loss of money. What bothered her the most was the money essentially saved to be spent on mandatory social obligations, such as the weddings of their children, would now be spent on her husband's recuperation—something the two of them hadn't 'planned'. Expenditure on saving a life is always seen as a liability and not as an investment.

Such is the irony. So, she had scowled at her children for booking a private room at the hospital for their father, lamenting that such *luxury* was beyond their means. It had offended the children.

'What are you saying, Ma,' her daughter looked surprised.

'There isn't much of a difference in the prices of a joint and a private room. We can afford that,' her son chipped in.

'Afford…do you even know where we are coming from? It is our hard-earned money…we can't be extravagant. If you feel ashamed asking the doctor to allot to us a shared room, let me speak to him.'

'And you will tell him what? What reason will you give him?' Asked her son with a tinge of irritation.

'I will tell him that we are Kashmiri Pandits. We are migrants. We don't have so much money.'

'Migrants! But, Ma… it happened almost three decades ago. We are financially stable now. Let us not discuss it further,' her daughter interrupted.

'It is pointless talking to both of you. You have no idea what kind of work your father did after he lost his job. But you seem to have no respect for that. Let me speak to your father. I am sure he, too, would agree with me. You don't get into this,' she said curtly.

As the logical arguments failed to pacify Mrs Kaul, her children left her alone. That was why she sat on the cold aluminium chair amid strange faces, clutching her bag tightly. The fuchsia sari, part of her wedding trousseau, picked randomly on that fateful evening in Srinagar, had been suitably transformed into a useful accessory. But its usefulness didn't make it significant until this moment of retrospection when she recalled the conversation she had with her husband on the day she wore the sari for the first time during their honeymoon. They had envisioned a beautiful life together. He had promised her many things... many...

'Mr Kaul, can you hear me?' asked the doctor. He nodded his head.

'Good. So, do you recognise her?'

His eyes squinted slightly. 'She is my wife.'

'Excellent!'

'Can you move your right hand?'

He struggled initially, but then lifted it up a bit.

'Very good. You seem to be doing fine. You will be under observation for the next 72 hours. We will let you know after that.'

She looked at his swollen face, puffy eyes and the white stubble scattered across his face like thin snowflakes, and smiled, without revealing her concerns. After they narrated him the sequences of events that landed him here, he looked worried. In a measured tone, he asked how much did it cost. A pregnant silence descended in the room.

'You don't have to worry about it now,' said his son. Silence again...

He looked at his wife as if trying to read her face. Her expressions. Her emotions. She didn't utter a word. The children were unnerved.

Suddenly, a smile crossed her lips.

'You remember, on our honeymoon you had said that one day we will go on a holiday and stay in a five-star hotel. You didn't have money then. So, let's presume that we are on a vacation. See, it is a nice, cosy room, with a television and a fridge too. We don't have a double bed though—I will manage on the couch. Don't think about money. Think of this as our first vacation together. The one we could never plan.'

Artichoke

Tammy Armstrong

Some things had happened lately. Not all of them good. So, when I'd said yes to Rome before knowing what Hollis's plans were, I was only thinking about bringing us back into balance. I was only thinking about letting us start again.

Of course, if we'd been getting along better, I might have realised this trip was not for mending broken parts but for research. Because it was always for research. Something else to tick off on Hollis's way to tenure. This one would be in search of the painter Caravaggio. There'd be a conference paper in the end, Hollis had said, tentatively titled, *Caravaggio: Scatological Imagery and Renaissance Humanism.* Or something like that.

But if *I* had to say where we first found Caravaggio in Rome that time, it would have been at a small *trattoria*, just off the Piazza Navona. We ate there because Hollis had insisted that we could not, absolutely not, eat *on* the Piazza. 'We would,' he'd said sternly, 'be cheated.'

Instead, paddocked into a narrow open-air patio, we sat at round tables with wobbly rattan chairs, far enough away from the Piazza to avoid being cheated, but near enough to watch the square's drama unfold. After a long first day battling crowds, I was content to just sit there and nurse my glass of Barbera, chosen for the price and because it was inky in the falling light. To my surprise, it tasted like cherry and red fruits turning. It tasted like cinnamon and something that reminded me of my mother's kitchen in early autumn.

While Hollis deciphered the menu, my attention strayed to the street hawkers roaming the square and to the luminescent balls some were ricocheting off the cobblestones. Lit up and spacey-blue, the toys hovered in the purpled sky for some seconds before floating back down into the hawkers' waiting hands. In between bounces, these men, some of them very young, would edge up to the groups of tourists half-gazing at the oscillating lights as they ate their waffle cones of gelato. Everyone, I noticed, seemed to be buying gelato from a man with a pushcart parked beneath a street lamp at the other side of the square. In the fading light, he looked very much like a minor celebrity.

From the patio, a cluster of these tourists' voices now cried and crouped and crowded the air as they argued over the best way to pronounce *stracciatella*.

'Strack-e-tella—like Nutella,' one of them said between licks.

'Naw, Jim. It's more like starchy-i-tell-ya. I think that's how that guy in the shop called it.'

Someone else, a woman with a high-pitched giggle, called over the group. 'Y'all just call it chocolate chip at home anyways!'

This sent a wave of big laughter through them as they moved on across the square, the balls of blue light, still falling back to earth and the hawker's waiting hands, now forgotten.

I glanced over at Hollis, knowing his face would be wrinkled with distaste for his fellow traveller, especially middle-aged men in Disneyland t-shirts and flip-flops. And then I turned my attention back to my glass of Barbera and the square, where the Fontana dei Quattro Fiumi's bottom-lit travertine rocks illuminated the river gods. Along these cobblestones, still wet where some children had been splashing earlier, the puddles caught and held the floating lights and those from neighbouring restaurants, making everything swimmy and strange. Just a feet from the dampness, a young man peddled selfie sticks, acrylic scarves and more glowing toys while another rearranged tripods and cheap leather goods on a worn tarpaulin.

'All they're doing is harassing people,' Hollis sighed, watching a hawker laden with knock-off handbags pass by our table. 'It's hard enough walking around here, bumping into crowds, let alone these guys selling junk. Something should be… ' But he left *the should be* unsaid.

Maybe Caravaggio would have painted these vendors, I thought. Maybe he would have captured their broken shoes, their worn jean cuffs and bloodshot eyes. And he would have emphasised this kind of early darkness that hides somethings while bringing other things to the foreground. In fact, I thought, *all of this* could be a Caravaggio painting. I drank some more wine. Now it tasted like liquorice and mushrooms.

'Caravaggio came to Rome when he was 21,' Hollis said, having forgotten the hawkers and tourists for now, 'after injuring a police officer in Milan. Piazza Navona was one of his haunts.'

I'd read something of this on the flight, over Hollis's shoulder.

'He once beat up a waiter. Right here!' Hollis continued, knocking on the table, 'Because he didn't like how his artichokes were cooked.'

When our waiter returned, the one who spoke in a formal but unenthusiastic kind of English, I ordered *carciofi alla Romana*, Roman-style artichokes, *linguine all'astice*, because I couldn't remember the last time I'd eaten lobster, and another glass of Barbera. Hollis raised an eyebrow at the expense but said nothing. He, of course, ordered something monkish and understated. *Spaghetti al pomodoro*, which was just spaghetti and tomato sauce, and a cappuccino, despite the waiter's disapproving grimace.

When the food arrived, Hollis took up his fork and twirled his pasta tightly over the tines. At the next table, a man leaned deeply over his own steamy plate. Cupping his hands toward his face as though he were drinking from a stream, he inhaled the savoury air above the dish. When Hollis wasn't looking, I leaned over my own plate and breathed my artichokes' herby warmth.

'Once, Caravaggio ordered eight artichokes in l'Osteria del Moro.' Hollis continued. 'They came in one dish. Some with oil. Some with butter. But they should have been served separately, see? Caravaggio was so pissed at this that he threw the dish at the waiter and pulled out a sword.'

'He must have really loved artichokes,' I said, forking another bite of mine into my mouth. It was soft enough to eat with a spoon. I closed my eyes, chewed slowly. Mint and olive oil. A slick of wine.

'He wasn't mad at the waiter's rudeness,' Hollis continued. 'He was mad because he hadn't taken the artichokes seriously. The waiter had *disrespected* the artichokes.'

'Do you want to try one? An artichoke?' I asked, edging my plate a little closer to his elbow. He slurped up another forkful of spaghetti, eyeing the artichokes standing on their stems.

'No, I don't think so. No. Heartburn.'

'That's fine then.'

To better enjoy the warm near-dark air, scented now with car exhaust and garlic, I let my pashmina slip from my shoulders. I liked how the Italians did this—ate a meal. I liked how they didn't bring ice in my water. They didn't leave sticky condiment bottles on the table or stand behind me with a pepper grinder the size of a stair spindle, asking if I want more pepper on my pasta. They didn't offer grated parmesan for fish dishes or give you spoons when the cannoli should be eaten with your hands. And they didn't drink cappuccinos at nine in the evening. I liked these unspoken, semi-old-fashioned but easy-to-follow rules.

After dinner, we walked back through the web of streets to our spartan rooms above a shoe store in Campo de' Fiori.

Around us scooters buzzed past, doubling nuns and students with overstuffed packs. There was something about Rome's darkness, settling now between the buildings and the lights, that created a curtain where it almost felt that things could be said. Things could be known. The thick air quivered. Noises grew and diminished. I brushed my hand over the chipped-away corners of buildings where cars had missed the tight turn.

'This is where Caravaggio killed a man with a sword. Over a tennis game!' Hollis said, almost to himself.

'I wonder where those street hawkers will sleep tonight, Hollis. I've read that many of them go to—'

'That light you see in his work? The kind that comes through grimy windows and dingy rooms? He called it God's light.' Hollis glanced at me, 'Amazing, eh?'

'It's something...' But I had nothing really to add.

We walked on. Past an alley. Overflowing dumpsters. Whippy cats. A church wall scribbled with graffiti. Soggy plastic bags. Dismantled bicycles. A truck beeping erratically as it backed up.

In the morning, Campo de' Fiori had transformed itself into a buzzy and bright open-air market. There were stalls arranged with spices by the weight, pencil-thin asparagus, strawberries from Terracina, flowers clubbed together with twine, trimmed and washed greens, bags of cipolline onions, sun-dried tomatoes, ham with fennel and boar salami. And there were Caravaggio's beloved artichokes, already cleaned and accompanied by a few herb sprigs. Even the wild chicory was neatly trimmed from its soily roots. All the dirt and darkness that Caravaggio loved, erased. There were also stands selling souvenir food. Fluorescent limoncello in violin-shaped bottles and bags of multicoloured, penis-shaped pasta, gimmicks that I thought Caravaggio might have appreciated, but Hollis did not.

We passed quickly through the market without buying anything. At its edge, three dogs slept in thin capes of light, their lean sides rising and sinking rapidly. Light coppered an upstairs window. A pot of red geraniums grew. Pigeons cooed from the burnt-tile roofs.

On our walk the night before, Hollis had insisted that we leave the apartment early in the morning because, despite jet lag, we needed to *beat the crowds* at the Contarelli Chapel. 'We need to get there first,' he'd said. So, we set out early morning for Piazza Navona as an alley cat might, lilting and drifting, keeping to the sides of buildings. Despite this, we were soon swept up in the crowds of backpacks, sun hats, guidebooks and telephoto lenses. The tour groups were already at the chapel, their coloured flags erect and waving as though preparing for a crusade. And while I tried to manoeuvre around the groups, politely mumbling, *scusi, scusi, scusi*, Hollis, looking neither left nor right, closed the space between himself and the three Caravaggio's dedicated to the life of Saint Matthew.

When I finally reached the trio of nearly life-sized paintings, there was something decidedly real and unreal about them. They had, in their way, a seedy sort of holiness bled through with Caravaggio's signature light. But what startled me most was their subjects and my familiarity with them. Their faces were the faces of the tourists milling around. The same ones forgetting to whisper or turn off their camera flashes. They were the faces of the street hawkers and those buying gelato from the man with the cart. They were just ordinary people in extraordinary moments.

Hollis stood now beside a little machine, which visitors kept feeding with one-pound coins so that spotlights in the ceiling would reveal the paintings. He dropped a coin into the slot, and I could see that this sort of illumination was just theatrical enough to impress him. Dark then light. Dark then light.

But all the marble, sculptures and gilding were weighing me down. Jet lag had settled into the base of my skull, and Rome suddenly felt imposing—all its opulence, flood-lit domes and subterranean secrets. I needed fresh air.

I sidled my way over to Hollis, who was furiously jotting notes into his black Moleskine. As the spotlights came on again, I saw that he'd forgotten to shave.

'I'm going over to that little coffee shop. The one near the Pantheon? The one with the potted palms at the door?'

Hollis nodded but didn't look up from his notes.

On my way out, pushing against the crowds, I passed a security guard chastising a woman for eating a granola bar in the chapel. A spark of sun caught on the wrapper's foil as she slipped the half-eaten evidence back into her handbag.

I found it easily. The coffee shop. Right on the Piazza del Pantheon. Rather run-down on the outside, dated, but crowded with mid-morning business. Wading into the line to the left of the door, I ordered from a humourless cashier.

'*Granita di caffè con panna, por favore,*' I said, because I'd been studying the board while waiting my turn and felt confident these words might roll out of my mouth crisp and curled the right way. And then, in a panic, thinking that this—my only chance to speak—was passing me by, I said too loudly, '*Stracciatella. Stracciatella. Anche.*' I waited for the cashier to give me an appreciative smile at my off-the-cuffness. Instead, he gave me a chit and jerked his head toward the other side of the room, where the coffee grinder roared and the barista worked amidst clouds of steam and the hiss of foaming milk.

The *caffe granita con panna* came in a tall glass with a long-handled spoon. The gelato came in a cone. With my handbag slipping from my shoulder and both hands full, I made my way back through the crowd, *scusi, scusi, scusi*, until I reached the exit. I found a concrete planter outside the door that held only a small palm, leaving just enough room for me to perch on its edge with my mid-morning findings. I tried the *granita* first. A bracing hit of slushy espresso. Icy and sweet. And then whipped cream, soft and plain. Rome will taste like this in my mind forever, I thought, as the sun warmed my face. I liked the plant pot I'd found. No one took any notice of me. Closing my eyes, I took another spoonful, reminding myself to save a bit for Hollis, if he should come around.

While I ate, the crowds moved in and out of the Pantheon to their varying rhythms. I watched those on two-wheeled Segways, and those hand in hand, and those following a tour group's scarlet flag, and those climbing out of horse-drawn carriages. I watched an elderly lady with a squeaky shopping trolley stacked with bread yell '*Va via! Va via!*' to a man insisting that she buy the bouquet of wilted roses he held between his filthy hands. And I watched Hollis come towards me through the square, scattering pigeons like folding fans as he sidestepped the tangle of tourists. His eyes only on the small space I'd claimed for myself beside the stunted palm.

Just as he raised his hand to wave, I bit down into my gelato and waffle cone. *Stracciatella*, I said to myself, marveling for a moment at how the word lit up the world and softened its unseen corners. And then I waved back.

Sunday, Bloody Sunday

Vineetha Mokkil

In the Bakshi household, it's family tradition to drink together on Sunday evenings. When we were kids, Nikhil and I used to sit at the table, orange juice in hand, watching Ma and Papa clink their glasses. We had a guessing game going.

Guess what whiskey tastes like?

*Cow piss *Honey *Cough medicine.

Wine?

*Grape juice *Goat's blood *Gutter water.

Vodka?

*Acid *Oil *Lemon juice.

Whatever my pick, Nikhil would sound disappointed. 'Wrong!' he'd say, putting on a grown-up voice. 'You're such a baby, Tara.'

Ma and Papa have kept up the Sunday tradition all these years. No matter where Papa was posted—desert, mountain, glitzy metropolis or godforsaken outback—they clinked their glasses as the sun set on the week. Bahadur brings out the bottles and glasses promptly at 6. Whiskey and soda, gin and tonic, wine, vodka, ice cubes—check, check, check. Bahadur runs our household like a well-oiled machine. Papa's major-domo, Ma's man Friday, our devoted housekeeper-cum-handyman-cum-cook.

The Sunday in question, Bahadur served us our drinks in the living room. The light outside was fading. A chill crept into the air like a ghost. Ma wrapped a shawl around her shoulders. The burnt orange fabric was the same shade as the autumn leaves fluttering over our driveway.

Papa swigged his whiskey. 'Cheers, guys,' he grinned, raising his glass.

Nikhil proposed a toast. He was in a great mood. His internet start-up had caught some big-shot investor's fancy. There was no way but up for his business from here.

Everybody looked nice and relaxed. Even Rudy, our cat, forever the haughty overlord, purred like a well-fed baby from under the table. This was it. The perfect moment, the perfect season to break the news. I took a deep breath, dived in. I'd rehearsed my lines a million times.

'I'm seeing someone. From work.'

Ma's face lit up like a Christmas tree. Papa's grin grew wider.

'Dating a fellow officer?' Nikhil teased me. 'Don't you guys have a country to run?'

I ignored his snark. Ignored the panic bubbling up inside me.

'We met at the Academy in our training days. At Mussoorie.'

'Aww...How romantic!' Ma sighed.

'We're from the same batch…'

'The Indian Administrative Service—A Love Story,' Nikhil joked without smiling

'So, what's his name?' Papa's baritone filled the air. 'When do we meet him?'

'Invite him for lunch or dinner,' Ma smiled, making mental notes about the menu. 'Weekend, weekday, anytime.'

'What's the problem?' Nikhil asked, mistaking my panic for reluctance. 'Is he a vampire? A vegan?'

'Faizal's not a fussy eater. Feed him anything, no complaints.'

'Faizal?' Papa's smile vanished.

'Faizal Mohammed.'

Ma stiffened and folded her arms across her chest as if she needed protection from me.

'He's from Kashmir,' I said. 'His parents live there. No siblings. Poor thing's an only child.'

Nobody said anything. Nobody moved. My parents and my chatty brother turned to stone.

'He's a really nice guy,' I mumbled, hating myself for sounding defensive. Faizal was the gentlest man alive. He could calm down an angry mob anytime, keep his cool even when he was faulted for no fault of his own. He loved to quote Shakespeare and Faiz and Neruda and Dickinson. Recite verse after verse from memory.

Nikhil snapped out of his trance. 'So, you're dating him. It's not like you're getting married or anything.'

'We are,' I kept my voice steady. 'We want to…'

Rudy crawled out from under the table and climbed up to my lap. Rudy, my friend. Ally in all battles, bloody or not.

'You want to marry a Kashmiri!' Papa gagged on his whiskey as if it was hemlock.

'Please don't make it sound like a crime.'

Ma wept quietly. Nikhil leaned sideways and put his arm around her shoulders. I felt alone even if all four of us were in the room.

Rudy burrowed deeper into my lap, determined to stick by my side.

'We're not in a hurry,' I said. 'Meet Faizal when you feel like it. No rush.'

Papa scraped back his chair and stood up. He was a tall man. Six-foot-one. A fighter pilot who had trouble fitting into airline seats. A fighter pilot trained to see the world in black and white.

'You're making a terrible mistake.' His tone as grim as a judge's at a hanging.

'Faizal's not a jihadi,' I snapped at him. 'He's an IAS officer like me. He has a good heart. And a very sharp brain.'

Ma sobbed. She didn't bother to wipe away her tears.

'Is it because he's a Muslim?' I asked. 'All Muslims are terrorists?'

'I know Kashmir,' Papa gave me a pitying look. 'I know how Kashmiris operate.'

'That's so unfair!'

'Indians who hate India. Indians who badmouth the country every chance they get. You can't trust these people.'

'Faizal's not like that!'

'Dig deep and you'll see.'

Nikhil stared at me from across the table as if I were a nine-headed monster. Ma wept.

'Meet him before you make up your mind. Give him a chance, please.' My request hung between us—a rickety bridge no one would cross. I waited for a kind word, a whiff of compromise. In the end, I gathered Rudy in my arms and walked out. The house was very quiet, very still. My footsteps rang out like gunshots in the night when I went up the stairs.

There is a before and after in every life. That Sunday cleaved mine in two. Life before and life afterwards—two mismatched halves that would never form a whole. Conversations became a tightrope walk. At mealtimes, the air was taut with tension. Anything I said was open to misinterpretation. A word, a joke, even the simplest gesture could set off an explosion. Rattled, I retreated into silence.

In the mornings, I skipped breakfast and left for work early. Faizal was my oasis of calm. He spotted silver linings in the dark. His infinite, almost annoyingly saintly capacity for keeping the faith was stronger than my doubts. He swore the cold war at home would end soon. We started spending more time together after work. Coffee in our favourite café, walks in Lodhi Garden, the lush green refuge in the heart of Delhi's urban sprawl. The garden brought out the poet in Faizal—he burst into song in the bamboo groves, recited love poems before the Mughal emperors' magnificent tombs, kissed me in the rose garden, serenaded me under the sprawling oaks.

Time slowed down when I was with him. The sun shone bright, the sky blazed blue. But evening always deepened into night, and night brought me no comfort. At home, a strained silence reigned. Dinner was the worst. Ma picked at her food distractedly. Papa chewed on his rotis with barely contained rage. Nikhil plodded on like a mourner at a funeral.

Bahadur hovered around the dining table, fussing over us, worrying if the whole family was coming down with something serious. Rudy sat at my feet, gazing at me with adoring eyes. I smuggled some fried fish to him. He arched his back, rubbed up against my legs and expressed his eternal gratitude. He was easy to please.

Sleep was a major casualty of our cold war. I tried everything—drinking herbal teas at bedtime, listening to soothing soundtracks (the song of the sea, the whisper of the wind), even counting sheep, clichéd as it is. Nothing helped. I was up all night, tossing and turning, stumbling out of my room like a sleepwalker at first light.

One night, tired of sparring with insomnia, I decided to go for a walk. A full moon hung in the sky. Stars blinked. Rudy came running to me, sensing my plan to step out. Wherever I was headed, he would follow. I slid back the bolt on my door. I jiggled the handle. Once, twice, thrice. The door wouldn't budge. Rudy butted his head against the door, sniffed at it, ran around the room in circles. He was as frustrated as me.

We gave up on our walk. All night, the door stayed shut. When sunlight started to trickle in through the curtains, I heard a soft click—the sound of a key turning—someone tiptoeing around, the sound of my door being unlocked. I froze. For the first time in my life, I was zapped by fear in my own house.

When I went down for breakfast with Rudy at my heels, Nikhil was huddled on the couch, his nose buried in the newspaper. Ma and Papa were out on the lawn, striking yoga poses, basking in the honeyed morning light. Bahadur brought me a cup of tea. Asked me if I'd slept well.

'I'm under house arrest,' I said. 'How can I sleep well?'

Bahadur made a quick exit. If a fight was brewing, he wasn't going to get caught in the cross hairs. Taking sides was a dangerous business, and Bahadur was a careful man.

'Why lock me up?' I raised my voice. 'Was that your idea?'

Nikhil looked up at me from his newspaper. His chin was covered in stubble. Dark circles shadowed his eyes. 'Don't yell at me, Tara,' he said. 'I have a headache.'

'What's next? Armed guards? Cops chasing after me on the street?'

'Stop it,' he said, massaging his temples. 'Your door's jammed, we'll get it fixed. End of story.'

I didn't have the stomach for a fight, so I backed away. Nikhil went back to reading the paper, and I headed to work. All day, a niggling feeling—fear, worry, a whiff of sadness— trailed after me like a shadow. Faizal's jokes didn't make me laugh. The future was a maze. Navigating it, even with Faizal by my side, looked like a hopeless business.

Weeks of strained silence at home, weeks of tightrope walking, and then the wind changed direction without warning. When I walked into the house on a Friday evening, Ma and Papa were grinning like children. They were dressed in their best, and Bahadur had cooked up a feast. Nikhil was home too. Talk and laughter and friendly banter drifted in the air.

Relieved, I sat down to dinner. Ma served me an extra helping of kheer. She'd made the dessert, my favourite, herself. We ate in peace. Chatted like we used to. Papa laughed at his own jokes. Nikhil and I pulled his leg. For an hour, I convinced myself that peace had returned. For an hour, I tricked myself into believing we had gone back to being the way we were before I took Faizal's name on a Sunday evening and the walls closed in on us.

When Bahadur came in to clear the table, Papa and Nikhil made a strategic exit from the room.

'Stay,' Ma smiled at me from across the table. 'Let's talk.'

Lulled by the feast and glasses of red wine, I leaned back in my chair. Ma spoke softly, strung her words together with care. The Kohlis—General Kohli and his wife, golfer and philanthropist, Sunita Kohli—had come by the house that evening. Their son, Vikas, was a heart surgeon who was famous for saving lives in San Francisco. A fine young man with an excellent pedigree. A green card holder. A respected member of the Asian-American community.

'A perfect match,' Ma smiled. 'You two would make a great couple.'

And then it dawned on me that nothing had changed. We were still stranded on opposite shores. The evening had been an illusion, a conjurer's trick to reel me in. A prelude for this proposal. A means to an end.

'He's not Faizal,' I explained. 'And Faizal's the only man I want to be with.'

Ma kept at it. A stream of advice, followed by angry tears and a bitter speech forged from disappointment. Papa was counting on me to make the right choice. Nikhil expected better from me. How could I be so stubborn? How could I humiliate my family this way?

I didn't tell Faizal about the heart surgeon. The Kohlis and their son had nothing to do with us. They were not part of our story. I didn't tell Faizal about my locked door either. His peace of mind was not mine to wreck.

We spent lunch hour together at office, took off for our walks in the evenings, caught a movie or a concert on the weekends, went book shopping at Midland, a landmark etched as clearly as the Qutub Minar on the mental map of the city's booklovers. The store had an impressive collection. The owner, soft-spoken and balding Rainaji, would dig up any book you demanded like a magician on stage. He chatted with all his customers. He knew the regulars by name.

A bookstore is the last place you expect to see spies at work. A strip joint or a pub with poor lighting, no surprises there. But Nikhil picked Midland to spy on Faizal and me. There he was, my lanky brother, dressed in a white shirt and jeans, peering at us from behind a stack of books, his gaze following us like a laser beam. A minute later, he was gone. Poof! A puff of smoke. A lightning flash. A pain in the neck. I would've laughed it off if I didn't know for sure that my brother never walked into bookstores, never read for pleasure even if a book jumped into his arms and begged to be read.

I was tempted to confront him. Order him to back off. But things were so tense at home, the peace—or what passed for it—so fragile, I chose not to make it worse by questioning him. I kept an eye out for him wherever we went. He could be trailing after us on the streets, driving at a discreet distance, mapping the routes we took. He could be hiding behind a bush or a giant oak in the garden, making notes about our evening stroll. The vigil was exhausting. I couldn't let my guard down even for a minute.

There was good news on the night-time lockdown though. Nervously, I tried my bedroom door every night. Miraculously, it swung open, letting me breathe easy. Ma and Papa kept conversations with me to a minimum. There were no heart to hearts, but the angry tears and accusations slowly dried up. Nikhil started to thaw too. Sometimes he shared a story about his day with me at the dinner table. Sometimes he cracked me up with a joke.

'Told you things would work out,' Faizal said. 'Give it time, my love. Just give it time.'

My heart stopped fluttering like a panicky bird. The days stopped weighing down on my head. The nights stayed the same though. In spite of my pleas, sleep refused to return.

One night, I was hunched over my desk, checking a file I'd brought home from work. A knock on the door made me jump. Rudy rushed to the door before I got there.

'Hey! It's me,' Nikhil's voice, a whisper, a reassurance.

I let him in. Rudy settled down at the foot of my bed, at ease.

'Ma sent this up,' Nikhil handed me a glass. 'Warm milk with saffron.'

'Thanks!'

'Guaranteed to put you to sleep.'

'We'll see,' I said, desperate to trust Ma's remedy.

Nikhil didn't stick around to chat. Long day at work, he was dying to go to bed. We said goodnight and I shut my door. Rudy purred softly from his perch.

I stayed up for another hour—checked my file, waded through a swamp of officialese and made sense of it. The night was quiet. No roar of traffic, no blaring horns or alarms. The silence was a balm. An invitation to drift off to sleep if ever there was one. I put away my papers and switched off my reading lamp. Rudy leaped into my lap, made me lose my balance and sent the glass of milk crashing to the floor. Before I could say a word, he crouched down and lapped up the milk, his pink tongue darting in quick bursts till the floor was wiped clean.

'Rudy,' I bent down to pat his fluffy head. 'Silly boy, Rudy.'

He purred and purred, and rolled over on his back. Milk was bliss. He was a good boy, easy to please.

I left him there, on the floor, and headed to the bathroom. Sleep or no sleep, a warm bath always made me feel better. Minutes later, when I came back into the room, Rudy was curled up on the floor at the exact spot where I had left him. But he wasn't moving. Or purring. Or giving me goofy looks. His eyes were shut tight and his body had turned an alarming shade of purple. I knelt down and scooped him up in my arms. He was so cold and stiff, so quiet.

'Rudy,' I called out to him, loud enough to wake my family, loud enough to wake the whole town.

I cradled Rudy in my arms, rocking him gently like a newborn babe. I slid the bolt back on my door. Yanked the handle. Yanked it hard.

The door wouldn't open. The door wouldn't budge.

The Crossing

Vrinda Baliga

What does it look like, this border on the open seas? You imagine a vast wire fence, bristling with barbs, anchored magically atop the waves, rising and falling with the heaving waters. You have been seeing variants of this image for many nights now. In your nightmares, it lies in wait like a mythical beast of yore for you to draw near so it can rip you apart with its clawed tentacles.

There are 50 of you in the cargo hold of the rickety old boat, crammed into a place that would have been snug for even a quarter of that number. The waves are high and choppy. Babies and young children wail their despair, but the adults among you, equally helpless, have, by now, learned to ignore their cries. When someone among you throws up, no apologies are made to those of you the vomit spews on. The time for such niceties is past, and personal boundaries have long evaporated in the heat of the crammed quarters. Indeed, it is difficult to know which of the numb limbs you are tangled in are your own.

Parcels, the handlers call you. Like anonymous packages wrapped in brown paper, each indistinguishable from the next, with neither name nor address stamped on to set you apart. Sometimes, they just refer to you as *cargo*, eliminating even the individuality implied by the plural.

'It won't be long now,' mutters a youth with the eyes of an old man.

This is his third attempt to get across. Twice, he has been turned back.

'They try to turn you back before you cross over,' he says. 'Before you become their headache.'

He dispenses nuggets like this with the authority of a veteran. One of the boats that attempted the crossing the previous week never made it, neither this way or that, he tells you. There were too many aboard, and the whole shebang capsized. He looks critically around as though contemplating which of you can be jettisoned if need be. You don't know his name. You haven't asked. Names have long ceased to matter—they are use-and-throw articles, of no value, easily discarded.

Your own name, the real one that belonged to the person you once were, has faded far into the recesses of your memory. Your family, too, is a mere blur of unfired neurons by now. Like an old poster, it has been plastered over with the new, changing faces you encounter every day. You can no longer picture the woman who had clung to your arm a lifetime ago, shouting, 'No, he's too young. He can't go alone. I won't let him!'

There was a time, not so long ago—no, eons ago—when with all the optimism and folly of youth, you had thought of this as an adventure. A brave, pioneering escapade, full of dangers and obstacles you would smite with your wit and strength and courage. A hero's journey.

You had all gone together to the agent—your father, mother, younger brother and you—your meagre possessions packed and ready. But the agent had counted the notes your father placed in his hand and shaken his head.

'This will cover the cost of just one,' he had said.

'But you told me…'

'That was eight months ago, brother,' the agent said bluntly. 'The rules of this game keep changing depending on the situation on the ground. I told you that so, didn't I?'

It had taken eight months to come up with the money.

'Smuggler,' your grandfather had muttered when your father had first told him about the agent and brought up the need to sell off a substantial portion of your land to pay for the trip. 'Trafficker,' he had hissed.

'Agent,' your father had insisted.

But your grandfather had turned away, shaking his head.

He's just bitter; he's too old to come. You immediately felt ashamed of the unworthy thought. But not too ashamed.

Had it all been for nothing then, the sale of land, the acrimony at home? But no, the agent had a suggestion.

'Send your eldest one,' he said, looking you over. 'He seems a strong lad. He'll find work easily enough. He'll be able to send for the rest of you in a couple of years.'

Your father stared at the notes in confusion. If you took the money back home, it would become the seeds that would lie unproductively in the belly of your rocky, barren land, waiting for the rains that would not come, it would become the tiles for your leaking roof, the part payment to the moneylender—some of the hundred things that needed to be bought or fixed or done just to keep going. It would be back to square one. Hell, you had never left that square all your lives. But here, in the agent's hands, perhaps...

'No, he's too young,' your mother protested, clinging to your arm. 'He can't go alone. I won't let him!'

'He's old enough,' your father declared.

There was no time for elaborate goodbyes. 'It won't be long,' you told yourself in the back of the agent's truck as you gazed at your family, growing ever smaller, already receding into your past. Your father looked determined, your mother was in tears. Your younger brother stood sullenly by their side, bitter at having been deprived of the journey you had both anticipated together.

'Don't worry, sister, I'll take good care of him,' the agent had promised your mother as he pocketed the money.

Two days later, you crossed a barbed fence in the dead of the night and then the agent was gone, replaced by a different one, who knew nothing of you or of the promise.

Still, those first couple of weeks hadn't been so bad. You were among people more or less like yourself, who spoke the same language, had the same mannerisms. Spirits, reasonably high.

'It won't be long,' you told each other and believed it.

Stories were exchanged amongst you, of friends and relatives and acquaintances who had gone before. The sister of an acquaintance in the neighbouring village whose family now had a house in a dreamy, leafy suburb. The distant cousin of a distant cousin who ran a successful business and sent money home every month. The village carpenter who had left, confident of making a fortune with his superior woodworking skills. And in the evenings, around motley campfires, there was always a game of cards to be enjoyed. And there was always someone among you who could catch a tune and sing some wrenchingly familiar song, conjuring up, for a few tantalizing moments, home in the back of a truck trundling down a dusty path.

But as the journey dragged on and on, the lilt eventually faded from your songs, and the vigour, from your eyes.

The handlers changed every few days, but they could all as well have been the same person for all the difference it made. They were all invariably gruff and harsh, a far cry from the agents who had been so full of rosy pictures and promises. They barked orders: 'Sit there.' 'Come here.' 'Don't do that!' 'Shut up!' You had to shell out money for every small luxury—a blanket, a smoke, some medicine. And if you asked questions, they were likely to be answered with a fist or a boot.

'It won't be long now,' you muttered now, more out of practice than conviction.

Darker stories began to be narrated—the niece who was lost en route, the infant who had never made it...and why had nobody ever heard from that village carpenter anyway? Was he dead, or pretending to be dead so he would not have to send money back home?

You would never do that, you promised yourself. You were determined to work hard, earn heaps of money and be reunited with your family. But, with every passing day, it became increasingly difficult to hold on to such intangibles as promises and determination.

There were days when you would have given anything just to return home.

Once, when you were huddled over a campfire, you spotted a map one of the handlers had carelessly left about. With your heart in your throat, you picked it up and slipped it under your clothing. For an entire hour you carried it close to your chest, right next to your wildly beating heart, till you got a moment to yourself. You opened the map out surreptitiously, one eye looking over your shoulder, and smoothed your hand over its crumpled body. The whole world lay in front of you. But where were you? You could have been anywhere on its flat surface—you hadn't the slightest clue where you could plant your finger to begin tracing the way back home.

The map merely showed you how lost you truly were. In the end, you put it back before it was even missed.

And always, a new border loomed on the horizon. One more hurdle to be crossed. Yet another test of your collective will.

Some of you fell behind, out of sickness or the inability to pay your way further. Others, equally bedraggled and glassy-eyed, took their place—more *parcels* from different countries, speaking other languages and dialects, all travelling on an invisible, underground conveyor belt, from destinations barcoded in the lines of their faces.

Even the amorphous identity of homogeneity melted away, and eventually the only lingua franca was the language of desperation, which, with a few minor hiccups and pidgin welds, you all understood.

There were new passes, identity cards, documents with your photos pasted over unknown names that were now your own. You were told who you were, where you were born and when. What you did for a living. Who your family was. What your dreams and aspirations were. The entire story of your life was dictated to you, and you were made to recite it again and again till you got it right. Your identity was hammered out on a forger's anvil and handed to you. But it was an evasive shapeshifter. It waited just long enough for you to allow yourself to occupy it before changing once again. One day you were a plumber, the next a student. A field-worker on some days, a factory-worker on others. You were altered from week to week, from place to place, from circumstance to circumstance, till you could hardly recognise yourself anymore.

There was only one constant—borders, fences, walls—no matter which way you turned or how far you went.

Sometimes, you were let through unmolested, with payment or favour discreetly changing hands. When there were no 'friends' about, you had to take detours—long deviations over mountains and across rivers. The rivers claimed some of you, the mountains more.

You remember the tattooed face of a middle-aged woman whose name you don't know. She had walked in silence for days in the bitter cold, hugging a bawling infant to her chest. Then, one day, she just sat down and refused to get up. You—all of you—left her there and moved on. There was no other option.

She had been with a family group—a man, an elderly woman and two young children.

'She was a cousin, a distant cousin,' the man said, resorting to the past tense already. 'We should have never brought her along, but she had nowhere else to go.' He seemed unable to stop talking. 'What should I do? Stay with her and let my own children die? We should have never brought her. But the agent said it would be easy...' And all the time, hot tears melted the frost on his cheeks in little rivulets of grief.

The woman didn't once call after you, beg you to stay. She sat there on the rock, still as a statue, nursing her infant at her breast.

And that night when after a long time you thought of your mother, it was that woman you saw in your mind instead. That was when you realised you couldn't remember your mother's face any more.

Perhaps it was then that some part of you gave up, when the individual 'you' stopped its flailing struggle to break through to the surface every now and then and allowed itself to be subsumed by the collective 'you'.

So, here you are, this is what it has all come to—this rickety boat and this tangle of limbs. If the boat goes down, who will the waters have swallowed? Will it only be a number, a collective statistic, that floats face-down on the surface of the ocean? Will your souls be as inextricably tangled in death as your bodies now are?

It won't be long, you repeat to yourself...yourselves. But, already, an eternity has passed.

What lies beyond this mythical border on the sea? What if the place you have run to is as bad as the place you ran from? What if, in its own different ways, it is worse even? What if you have been running around in circles all this while?

You find you can't summon the energy to care either way.

Contributors

Ameta Bal is a postgraduate in Fashion and English Literature. She has worked with *Indian Express*, *Hindustan Times*, *Marie Claire* and *Elle*, and alternated between living in Mumbai and Delhi multiple times. She is currently learning Korean, and spends her time gaming, watching and reading all things apocalyptic, while trying in vain to shun social media.

Anila SK is an international development professional with interests in writing and film-making. She has worked for several international development agencies, including the United Nations World Food Program in Sudan and the government of Sri Lanka. She has spent her time between India and Sri Lanka. She believes that living in two different countries and witnessing war, death and separation have shaped her perspectives of life.

Anjali Doney is a physicist-turned-teacher who writes when she can. She enjoys writing short stories, poems and articles, some of which can be found at medium.com/@anjalidoney. Kochi is home, but she currently lives in Bengaluru.

Camilla Chester has three successful self-published children's fiction novels: *Jarred Dreams, EATS* and *Thirteenth Wish*. Camilla was shortlisted in the 2015 New Author Prize run by The Literacy Trust, and her second book EATS received Highly Commended in Winchester Festival Funny Fiction Award 2017. In addition to writing, Camilla has a small dog-walking business, and lives with her husband and two children in Hertfordshire, England.

Geetha Nair G. is a retired professor of English from Thiruvananthapuram, Kerala. She has published several poems and short stories in both print and online magazines. She is a winner at the Rabindranath Tagore Poetry Competition, 2019. A collection of her poems, *Shored Fragments*, came out early this year. *Journeys Within*, another collection of short stories, is readying for release.

Helen Harris is the author of six novels and many short stories published in a wide variety of magazines and anthologies. She has travelled widely and taught creative writing in India and in the Middle East. Today, she lives in London where she has taught creative writing at Birkbeck, University of London, and started a life story writing programme for older people. She is currently working on a series of short stories set in the time of Covid.

Humra Quraishi is a Delhi-based writer-columnist-journalist. She has several publications to her credit, including two short story collections, *Bad Time Tales* and *More Bad Time Tales*. She has co-authored *Absolute Khushwant* and a series of writings with the late Khushwant Singh. One of her essays, 'The State Can't Snatch Away our Children', is part of the Zubaan published anthology, *Of Mothers and Others*.

Jayshree Misra Tripathi lived a nomadic life in diverse cultures from 1986 till 2015. Jayshree was in the print media in the late 1980s and has written from across three continents. She has also taught and examined English Language and Literature for the Diploma of the International Baccalaureate Organization. Her poetry and short stories were recently reviewed in The Sahitya Akademi's journal, *Indian Literature*. Jayshree continues raising awareness on adult literacy and women helping women, in India, with her project #HelpHerWalkForward.

Latha Anantharaman is a writer, editor and translator, now based in Palakkad, Kerala. Her columns on books, language, rural life and sustainable living have been published in *LiveMint*, *Business Standard*, *The Hindu* and *Business Line*. She writes travel articles for *Outlook Traveller* and reviews books regularly for *The Hindu* and *India Today*. She is the author of a short memoir about life in the country, called *Three Seasons* (2015), as well as a book about Tamil Nadu (2007). She has edited a brief history of Kalpathy agraharam (in press). 'The Very Narrow House' is her first work of fiction.

 **Meena Menon** is an independent journalist and former deputy editor, *The Hindu*. She is also a doctoral candidate in the School of History, University of Leeds, UK. She is the author of the books *Riots and After in Mumbai, Reporting Pakistan, Organic Cotton: Reinventing the Wheel,* and has co-authored *A Frayed History, the Journey of Cotton in India.* She is the recipient of several media fellowships and has been a journalist since 1984. The inspiration for the story in this anthology came from a paper by Shahnawaz Khan, a Kashmiri journalist who researched closed cinemas in Kashmir as part of a Sarai-Centre for the Study of Developing Societies (CSDS) short-term fellowship project in 2007.

 **Meher Pestonji** has been a freelance journalist since the mid-70s. She has a wide spectrum of interests, and has been a theatre critic, art writer, book review columnist, and written extensively on street children, housing rights for slum dwellers and anti-communalism issues. In 1999, she published her first collection of short stories titled *Mixed Marriage and other Parsi Stories.* She has to her credit two novels titled *Pervez* and *Sadak Chhaap.* Her play *Piano for Sale* opened at the

National Centre for the Performing Arts in 2005. Her second play, *Feeding Crows*, won the South India segment of the British Council/BBC Radio Playwriting Competition in 2008.

Rinita Banerjee is particularly fond of words. She is a writer (adult literary fiction) and translator (fiction for children, young adults and adults), and a copy editor for close to eight years. An avid reader and film enthusiast, she can also sing in four languages, including French. At one point, she was an English newsreader for the overseas audience at All India Radio's general news division. She has a Masters in English (concentration: American and British Literature) from the North Carolina State University (Raleigh, USA), and graduated with a Bachelors in Psychology from Lady Shri Ram, Delhi University.

Rochelle Potkar is an alumna of Iowa's International Writing Program (2015) and a Charles Wallace Writer's Fellow, University of Stirling (2017). Fictionist, poet, critic, curator, editor, translator and screenwriter, her book of haibun, *Paper Asylum*, was shortlisted at the Rabindranath Tagore Literary Prize

2020. Her poetry film, *Skirt*, features on Shonda Rhimes' Shondaland. *Bombay Hangovers* is her recent book, a collection of 16 short stories across caste, class and religion, set in Mumbai.

Sarah Robertson, former newspaper journalist and business editor, has taken a break from the corporate world to focus on her creative writing full-time. She divides her time between Scotland and London, and when she's not working, she enjoys free diving, motorcycles and walking her dog.

Shilpa Raina is currently working as an assistant editor with TV18 Broadcast Ltd (CNN-News18). She was the chief reporter at *Deccan Herald* and principal correspondent at Indo-Asian News Service. Her work has also been published in *The Hindu*, *The Indian Express*, and *TAKE on Art* magazine. Her first short story featured in the anthology *Once We Had Everything*.

Tammy Armstrong has published two novels and five books of poetry. Her first collection, *Bogman's Music*, was a finalist for the Governor General's Award. Her recent work has been a finalist for the National Magazine Awards, and has won the iYeats International Poetry Prize (Ireland), *Prairie Fire*'s Bliss Carman Poetry Prize, the Cafe Writers Poetry Competition (UK), and the *Well Review* Prize (Ireland), among other prizes. Her most recent poetry collection, *Year of the Metal Rabbit* (2019), was a finalist for the Atlantic Book Awards' J.M. Abraham Poetry Award and the Maxine Tynes Nova Scotia Poetry Award. She lives in Nova Scotia.

Vineetha Mokkil is the author of the short story collection *A Happy Place and Other Stories*. She received an honorary mention in the Anton Chekhov Prize for Very Short Fiction 2020, was shortlisted for the Bath Flash Fiction Award in 2018, and is the winner of the New Asian Writing Short Story Competition 2018. She was a nominee for *Best Small Fictions 2019*. Her fiction has appeared in *Gravel*, the *Santa Fe Writers' Project Journal*, *Barren* magazine, *Quarterly Literary Review Singapore*, *Asian Cha*, *Melbourne Culture Corner*, and in the anthology *The Best Asian Short Stories 2018*.

 **Vrinda Baliga** is the author of short story collections *Name, Place, Animal, Thing* and *Arrivals and Departures*. Her work has appeared in short-fiction anthologies—*The Best Asian Short Stories 2018* and *And Lately, The Sun*— and literary journals, such as *Asia Literary Review, Himal Southasian, The Indian Quarterly, New Asian Writing*. She has won prizes and recognition in the Bengaluru Review Short Story Competition 2020, Katha Fiction Contest 2017, the FON South Asia Short Story Competition 2016 and New Asian Writing Short Story Competition 2016. Vrinda lives in Hyderabad, India, with her husband and two children.

Acknowledgements

The Punch Magazine's call for short story submissions had received an overwhelming response from writers around the world. I thank the 18 women writers who are part of this anthology for their patience, as the pandemic delayed its release, and for their unwavering faith in us. I am grateful to Gulzar saab for his gracious endorsement.

Tultul Niyogi and Trisha Niyogi of Niyogi Books not only showed great interest in the anthology but also ensured that the publishing process was quite smooth. I thank them for their association and for their efforts to bring this book into being. Editor Upama Biswas and cover designer Misha Oberoi did their best, and I thank them.

The Punch Magazine, conceived as a collective, has been able to chart its own path, carve out its own distinct identity. This has been possible due to the efforts of all the contributors, curators, writers and readers who have engaged with the magazine ever since its inception in December 2016. They are many, and I thank each one of them. I also thank all the contributing editors and friends of *The Punch Magazine* for being around. Some of them include RM, RG, CPS, IP, HQ, JMT, SS, PKM, SD, SS, SG and AT. Special thanks to Nawaid Anjum, who has been the moving spirit behind the magazine.